T0167969

THOMAS L. SYNNOTT:
The Career of a Dublin Catholic 1830–70

Maynooth Studies in Local History

GENERAL EDITOR Raymond Gillespie

This is one of the new pamphlets published in 1997 in the Maynooth Studies in Local History series. Like earlier titles in the series, published in 1995 and 1996, each study is derived from a thesis completed in connection with the Maynooth M.A. course in local history.

The localities studied are defined not by administrative boundaries but by the nature of the community bonds which shaped people's experiences in the past, both holding them together and driving them apart. Ranging across family, village, parish, town, and estate, the pamphlets investigate how people in these varied communities lived out their lives and responded to changes in the outside world.

These Maynooth Studies in Local History explore the richness and diversity of the Irish historical experience, and in doing so present local history as the vibrant and challenging discipline that it is.

Maynooth Studies in Local History: Number 14

Thomas L. Synnott:

The Career of a Dublin Catholic 1830–70

Bob Cullen

IRISH ACADEMIC PRESS

Set in 10 on 12 point Bembo by
Carrigboy Typesetting Services, Co. Cork
and published by
IRISH ACADEMIC PRESS LTD
Northumberland House
44, Northumberland Road, Ballsbridge, Dublin 4, Ireland
and in North America by
IRISH ACADEMIC PRESS LTD
c/o ISBS, 5804 NE Hassalo Street, Portland, OR 97123

© Bob Cullen 1997

A catalogue record for this title
is available from the British Library.

ISBN 0-7165-2630-1

All rights reserved.
No part of this publication may be
reproduced, stored or introduced into a
retrieval system, or transmitted, in any form
or by any means (electronic, mechanical,
photocopying, recording or otherwise),
without the prior written permission
of the copyright owner.

Printed in Ireland
by ColourBooks, Dublin

Contents

Acknowledgements

I would like to gratefully acknowledge the assistance of the following: Dr. Raymond Gillespie and Dr. Jacqueline Hill for their patient guidance, encouragement and support.

The staff of the following institutions for their courteous assistance: Gilbert Library, Holy Faith Archives, Dublin City Archives, Dublin Diocesan Archives, National Library of Ireland, National Archives of Ireland, Representative Church Body Library, Trinity College Map Library and Maynooth College Library.

Professors Emmet Larkin and Donal Kerr, David Sheehy, Seamus Cummins, Barry McGettigan and Mark Fottrell for their help and encouragement.

My children, Philip, Stephen, Natalie, and especially my wife, Nicole, for their unfailing support.

My colleagues in the Maynooth M.A. local history class of 1994–6.

Introduction

Thomas L. Synnott first came to my attention when reading correspondence in the Archbishop Murray papers relating to the great famine, 1845–50.[1] Mary Purcell drew the attention of historians to this famine correspondence in an article entitled 'Sidelights on the Dublin Diocesan Archives', in which she referred to the appointment of Synnott as administrator of the relief money sent to the Catholic archbishop of Dublin from around the world.[2] Over seventy of the moving letters there, from famine-stricken areas in the west of Ireland, were addressed to Synnott. These letters are an important primary source for our understanding of his role in famine relief.

The aim of this pamphlet is to focus not only on Synnott's involvement in the distribution of the Murray fund for famine relief, but on an overall interesting career spanning the period 1830 to 1870. These parameters are determined to some extent by the sources which have made possible this study of a rather elusive historical figure. Hopefully, and very probably, they coincide with the more important events of his career. A study of the interaction between Synnott and the different communities with which he was involved, will, it is hoped, help to form a coherent picture of him.

The first part will look at his early years as a resident and somewhat comfortable shopkeeper in the north Dublin parish of St. Paul's. It will also deal with his increasingly public life first as a officer of the local vestry and in the early 1840s as an elected guardian of the North Dublin Union. This local prominence led to success beyond St. Paul's parish. His wider political involvement from the time of his appointment as high constable and billet master to Dublin corporation will also be considered. Since one can only know Synnott in the political, social and economic context of his time, the chapter will look briefly at the background here, especially the flowering of the Dublin Catholic middle-class on the coat-tails of Daniel O'Connell's leadership and achievements. The second part will focus on Synnott's involvement in relief work during the great famine. This was not limited to his work with Archbishop Murray, which came about because of earlier work as secretary to various national voluntary relief committees.[3] Apart from brief references this topic has not received much attention from historians. The focus here will be on the interaction between Synnott and Murray, and with the other relief committees of which he was secretary. Thirdly we will look at Synnott's work as governor of a Dublin female prison which covered a period of some twenty years, and which was the setting for a tragic end to what had promised to be a highly successful career. Again the focus will be on Synnott's relations with the various structures connected to this prison, both from within and outside the prison. Emphasis will be placed on the imprisonment of Margaret Aylward (foundress of a children's orphanage and of the Holy Faith religious order) while Synnott was governor there, and the implications this had for his career.

The value of this study is that it is the story, told for the first time, of a particular individual from our past in the context of his community. Synnott perhaps is one of many such relatively minor historical figures whose story is there to be told. Reference has been made to him in some historical works, but only with minimal detail to elucidate a point about another person or event. Apart from Mary Purcell's reference to him which is very brief, he gets some attention from one biographer of Margaret Aylward.[4] Canon O'Rourke's nineteenth century history of the famine acknowledges Synnott as the secretary of the Mansion House Committee, and credits him with having produced an analysis of the returned questionnaires giving details of the extent of the potato loss in Ireland in 1845.[5] He also features in Desmond Bowen's study of 'souperism' during the great famine.[6] A recent history of the famine years by Donal Kerr refers to his role as administrator of the Murray fund, and provides a brief biographical footnote.[7] Murray's role in famine relief has also been referred to by David Sheehy.[8] The little attention given to Synnott is rather surprising given his important role in famine relief. While work has already been done on the Catholic middle-class in mid-nineteenth-century Dublin,[9] a study of this development through the eyes and actions of one of its more successful members will it is hoped contribute to the general understanding of that period.

Synnott's early career before the famine period, especially the 1830s, is somewhat sketchy because of the limited available sources. For the social, geographical, economic and political background much dependence has been placed here upon contemporary maps and histories, directories and parliamentary papers. Direct references to Synnott's early career are scarce and mainly to be found in contemporary newspapers. The minutes of St. Paul's vestry make brief mention of his role in the work of the local vestry. The board of guardian minutes of the North Dublin Union for the 1840s are more expansive on Synnott's district in Dublin and especially on his role as a guardian there from 1839–43. Contemporary newspapers have also been an important primary source here.

It was his involvement in public institutions, for which the sources are relatively plentiful, that makes possible a study of this rather elusive figure. This is particularly the case for his years as governor of Grangegorman female prison for which there are printed and manuscript records. These include the chief crown solicitor's papers in the National Archives, which included detail on the legal action taken by Synnott against the lord lieutenant for assault and wrongful dismissal in 1865. Particularly important was the discovery of a file on Synnott in the chief secretary's papers which contains over fifty manuscript and printed documents which refer to his career up to and beyond his dismissal from the prison service.[10]

The Dublin corporation archives have minute books of the Dublin municipal council, and of the board of superintendence which visited the city prisons. These include letter-books and prison governor journals all of which have been particularly helpful, especially on the imprisonment of Margaret Aylward in 1860 in Grangegorman Prison. The Holy Faith archives in Dublin also contain some manuscript and printed material on this *cause celebre*. Rena Lohan's study of Irish women prisoners and transportation in the nineteenth century provides much on Grangegorman Prison, although little on Synnott himself.[11]

A less clear picture emerges of his involvement in famine relief. Apart from the Murray papers and some references to Synnott in the relief commission papers, the dependence here is more on contemporary newspapers. However the value of this latter source is lessened by Murray's reluctance to publicise the distribution of subscriptions sent directly to him.[12] There is very little manuscript material on the General Relief Committee (its full title was the 'General Central Relief Committee for all Ireland'). This was the third largest voluntary committee in Ireland during this famine. Nor is there much on the Indian Relief Fund. Synnott was centrally involved with these two committees. This means we are dependent on their printed reports and the glimpses provided by the newspapers of that time.

The study of the great famine edited by R. Dudley Edwards and T.D. Williams has been the accepted authority,[13] while C. Woodham Smith's account has had perhaps a wider and more popular appeal.[14] Mary Daly's short survey revised some of the widely-held views on the famine.[15] Donal Kerr's *A Nation of Beggars?* explores the relationship between priest and people in the famine years. Christine Kinealy's *This Great Calamity* focuses mainly on the role of the Poor Law in its alleviation.[16] J.S. Donnelly's study of the famine in the *New History of Ireland* provides background for this study of Synnott.[17] While most of these surveys make reference to the role of voluntary relief, they focus on the highly-profiled Central Committee of the Society of Friends, and somewhat less so on the British Relief Association. Little if any reference has been made to other national committees. This pamphlet tells the story of Synnott's work with these other national committees as well as his subsequent career as a prison governor, thus adding to our understanding of the social history of Dublin in the nineteenth century.

Synnott and St. Paul's:
The Early Years 1830–48

Thomas Lambert Synnott was born in 1810.[1] His birthplace has not been located, but we do know that from the early 1830s he lived in St. Paul's parish immediately north of the river Liffey on the west of the city of Dublin.[2] Most of his life from early adulthood was spent in Dublin. Six of his children were baptised in the Catholic chapel in St. Paul's parish.[3] A contemporary list of voters at parliamentary elections shows that his father voted as a freeman of Dublin in 1835 and 1837.[4] While this places the latter in Dublin from the early 1830s, it also suggests that he may have been a member of the established church. Almost all of Dublin's freemen at this time were Protestants.[5] However it is known from other sources that his son Thomas, if not a Catholic at birth, was certainly of that religious persuasion for most of his life.[6]

A brief look at the social and economic environment in which Synnott lived in the 1830s and 1840s should help to form a picture of him. Street directories link the Synnott family with Barrack Street and Ellis Quay in the parish of St Paul's from the 1830s.[7] This parish, now more commonly known as Arran Quay, was situated in the north western part of the city of Dublin (figure 1).

The population of the city had grown dramatically in the eighteenth century, to a large extent because of the migration of mostly Catholic poor from the neighbouring counties of Meath and Kildare into the city. This migration had gradually eroded the Protestant numerical dominance in the city.[8] The Protestant community in St Paul's had been eroded over the years, many of the wealthy among them moving to the more fashionable districts close to Sackville Street. An appeal for financial aid for St. Paul's Protestant schools in 1845 referred to the 'removal of the wealthy inhabitants from this once flourishing but now impoverished district'.[9] A government report on schools in St. Paul's parish in 1827 shows that in twenty-four of them the vast majority (67 per cent) were Catholic.[10] Many of the migrants in Dublin would have settled in the Barrack Street area which was close to the main arterial approaches to the city from the north through Dorset Street, Bolton Street and Capel Street, and from the west through Chapelizod.

The proximity of these access roads to Barrack Street would also partly explain the pressure placed on north-west Dublin in times of famine and fever. The main attraction of the area were the local hospitals which drew in fever-stricken labourers from outside Dublin in 1817.[11] The awful conditions in Barrack Street are graphically described in the government inquiry into this

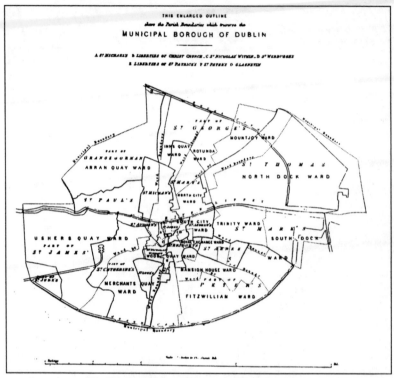

1. Location of St. Paul's parish. Index to the Townland Survey of County Dublin 1 : 126,720 (1888)

fever. During the cholera epidemic of 1832 St. Paul's parish received government aid of £100 up to 6 August to help fight it. In contrast, neighbouring parishes such as St. Nicholas Within and St. Michan received £30 and £422 respectively.[12] The relatively low per capita aid given to St. Paul's (Table 1.1) may have been due to the epidemic having had a smaller effect on that parish. The completed questionnaires returned from these parishes however vary in the detail given, and account must be taken of the possibilities of exaggeration in order to secure the money applied for.

Table 1.1 Relief given during cholera epidemic of 1832

Parish	Population (1831 census)	Amount of relief	Ratio of relief to population (£)
St. Paul's	10,570	£100	0.9
St. Nicholas Within	1,850	£30	1.6
St. Michan's	23,918	£422	1.8

(*Source for amount of relief:* Applications for Loans, Cholera Papers 1832–34, 4 N.A. 2/440/8)

2. 'Clearing-house for poverty and crime'. Ordnance Survey of County
Dublin 1 : 10,056, Sheet 18 (1843)

By the 1840s the landscape near Barrack Street had changed. The houses directly in front of the barracks had been replaced by an esplanade. The Synnott business at 61 Barrack St., described as just facing the clock in the barracks,[13] must have been included in the clearance to make way for the esplanade. Close by, the area near the old House of Industry now included the Richmond Female Penitentiary and the North Dublin Union workhouse, reflecting a huge clearing house for poverty and crime (figure 2).

Synnott was to spend much of his working life as an elected guardian of this workhouse and later as governor of the Penitentiary there.

Another significant change in the Dublin landscape in the nineteenth century, evident in the contemporary maps, is the increased number of Roman Catholic churches. St. Paul's Catholic church in Arran Quay stands out, a reflection of the growing middle-class Catholic population (figure 3).

The newspapers of the time provide snapshots of Synnott attending meetings in St Paul's church in the 1840s as for example in 1846 'to consider the great and hourly increasing distress of the poor of the parish.'[14]

Synnott in these years while he lived in the parish of St. Paul's was surrounded by poverty. It would appear however that he and his family lived in relative comfort. There is a memorial in the Registry of Deeds, Dublin, of a lease in 1835 of 59 Barrack Street,[15] granted to his father to which Thomas junior was himself a witness. The limited term (16 years) and the relatively high rent (£65) may be partly explained by the nature of his father's business (a vintner) and the proximity of the premises to the large barracks which provided a potentially large and regular custom. In spite of government efforts to control the trade, and especially the highly profiled and successful temperance crusade of the priest Theobald Mathew[16] from the 1840s, the Synnott family

3. St Paul's R.C. Church

appear to have maintained a degree of prosperity. The family's relative wealth is reflected in the family grave in Glasnevin cemetery in Dublin which is double-sized (eight by four feet) and surrounded by a foot high wrought iron railing.[17] Relative wealth for the Synnotts, it appears from the cemetery records, was no guarantee of longevity. What is striking about the Glasnevin register of burials for the extended family are the ages at death: seven out of sixteen were under three years of age, and eleven were under forty-six years of age.[18]

The Dublin street directories have much information on the relative wealth of St. Paul's parish for this period. For example, the type of business in Ellis Quay in 1850 which consisted of vintners, tavern-keepers, tobacconists, a watch and clock maker, and a wig manufacturer, can be contrasted with the wealthier Gloucester Street North with its prominence of barristers and solicitors (thirty-four out of forty-five houses). Religious affiliation is also discernible in the names of the residents, most in Ellis Quay being Roman Catholic while most of those in Gloucester Street North were (probably) Church of Ireland. The Royal Barracks influenced the economy in St. Paul's parish. Shaw's directory[19] for example shows various shops dealing in military ware. Local vintners and grocers like the Synnotts must also have benefited. It would appear from the Dublin directories that Synnott's father established his son as a grocer in 61 Barrack Street in 1835 while he himself first ran the vintner shop in number 59. By the 1840s the Synnott family had moved to nearby Ellis quay, where they and the extended family remained in the wine and grocery trade up to the 1880s (figure 4). By then Synnott had long since severed his connection with the business.

SYNNOTT AND THE VINTNERS

Contemporary newspapers of the 1830s report that a Thomas Sinnott (sic) of Ellis Quay was present at and took an active part in the vintners' association meetings.[20] The difficulty here is knowing which of the family is referred to. Both father and son shared the same first name, and the son's distinguishing middle name of Lambert does not appear in the newspaper reports of the vintners' association meetings. However although the son is described as a grocer in the directories, he may have had a license to serve alcohol. A significant number of grocers at the time were also licensed vintners. In one report[21] of a vintners' meeting criticism was made of the grocers who attempted to attract custom by presenting their premises as more suitable drinking places for the respectable citizens. Following a memorial[22] of Irish grocers in 1836 that part of the 1836 act prohibiting the sale of spirits by grocers was suspended.[23]

Even if it was Synnott's father who is referred to in the reports, the younger Synnott would have also shared in the concerns raised at their meetings. These included the perceived grievances and disabilities under which they laboured, especially the so-called Algerine act which removed licenses from

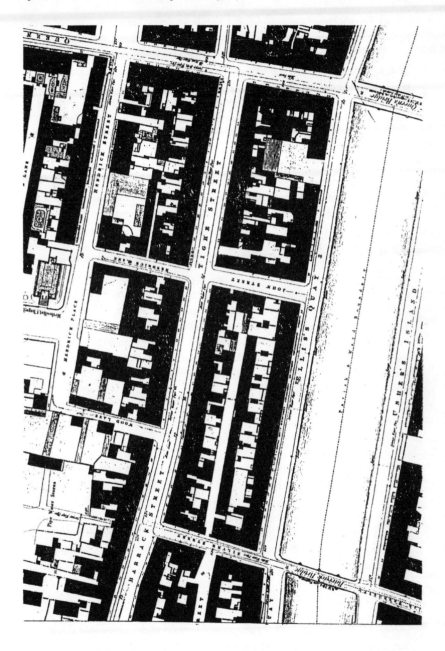

4. Ellis Quay. Ordnance Survey of City of Dublin 1 : 1,056,
Sheet 13 (1847)

vintners with three convictions for breaking drink laws.[24] At one of these meetings one of the Synnotts seconded a rather exaggerated motion describing this act as 'the most cruel and oppressive that ever disgraced the Statute Book of any country'.[25] From the speeches made at such meetings one gets the impression of a consciously powerful political lobby whose lofty assertions of being honourable and charitable (vintners funded an orphanage in Dublin at this time)[26] and the most moral of groups were an effort to counter the public perception of the drinking house as the occasion of prostitution and drunkenness. The point was made that if not encouraged by more enlightened legislation the trade would fall under the control of unlicensed houses where robberies and combinations were planned and loose women proliferated.

The Synnotts and the other vintners had also to contend with the increasing success of the temperance movement, a success due to Theobald Mathew in the late 1830s. The abstinence movement appeared to be very strong in the parish of St. Paul's which was represented by some 6,000 members of St. Paul's Temperance Society in a march of various abstinence societies through the city in March 1840.[27] The success of this movement and of government legislation is reflected in the decrease in the number of vintners in Dublin city in the 1840s: from 514 in 1840 to 228 by 1849.[28] (What effect they had on the number of unlicensed premises is not known.) Synnott's later political career was not negatively affected by the successes of the temperance movement, and might well have been helped by his links with the vintner/ grocery trade, most of whose members were in the liberal O'Connellite mould in the 1830s and 1840s.[29]

SYNNOTT AND ST PAUL'S VESTRY

The campaign of Daniel O'Connell for Catholic emancipation, which culminated in the passing of the Roman Catholic Relief act of 1829,[30] had given a new confidence to Irish middle-class Catholics which was reflected in public fora such as parish vestries. The vestry was an anomaly in that it was concerned with the spiritual and temporal life of the established church, and therefore (understandably) controlled to a large extent by its own members. At the same time it had civic responsibilities which went beyond the boundaries of its Protestant membership, but which were also largely in the control of Protestants. However, general vestries since the ending of the penal laws included all ratepayers and the number of Catholics attending those in the city increased in the 1830s.[31] St. Paul's general vestries in the late 1830s, frequently attended by Synnott, were sometimes so packed as to cause serious disruption of the meetings.

Parish officers were required by law to be members of the established church. This requirement was not always adhered to.[32] From the early nineteenth century Catholics were often appointed to such positions as applotter, parish constable and officer of health. Synnott's name appears at least twelve times between 1835–45 as attending vestries in St Paul's. He was elected an officer a number of times, as an applotter, a parish constable, and an officer of health.[33] Catholics however were excluded from the most important position in the vestry, that of church warden, although spasmodic attempts to have a Catholic elected to this post in Dublin vestries date back to the 1780s.[34]

The vestry minute books, despite their brevity, provide snapshots of the people of St. Paul's parish. There are also sometimes glimpses of major wider issues and how they were viewed, such as the cholera epidemic in 1832 with 'which Providence was pleased to visit us'.[35] One effect of the greater Catholic participation in general vestries was that they often became the forum for many of the political issues of the time. As the newspapers indicate, Synnott became a frequent attender at these meetings and was often centrally involved in local controversial issues.

On the 1 April 1839, a very unruly meeting took place in the overcrowded vestry room of St. Paul's. One of those present, Edward Brennan, objected to the appointment of Henry Price, a conservative Protestant, as a church warden and suggested that a liberal Protestant or a Catholic be elected instead. When reminded that, being a Catholic, he had no right to prevent the appointment of Price, Brennan replied that he would assert his right to do so in open (general) vestry. The open vestry attended by a crowd too large for the vestry room became unruly and Brennan proposed it be adjourned to the local school room. Price's answer was that Brennan was not a ratepayer and therefore was not entitled to move an adjournment. Synnott came to Brennan's support saying: 'I am a ratepayer, and will move the adjournment'. Price's response was that the governors of the school would not allow the school to be used. Brennan then threatened to move the appointment of another chairman. On being told he was not entitled to do this, Synnott himself proposed that John Burke take the chair. The chairman, Rev J. H. Lefanu, attempted to proceed with the vestry business against a noisy but good humoured crowd, one faction of which was led by Brennan and Synnott who continued to argue that the meeting should be adjourned. Unable to control the meeting, Lefanu finally got up and left the room in haste. Price moved a vote of thanks to the chairman for his very proper and impartial conduct in the chair! This provoked even more noise, derision and confusion, during which Burke ascended to the table and took the chair. Price then sent for the police who, although they came, remained outside the vestry. An adjourned meeting did take place some days later with Burke in the chair and Brennan as secretary. Among the resolutions unanimously agreed to was the following which was seconded by Synnott:

> That inasmuch as the Chairman, the Rev Mr. Lefanu, refused to take
> the opinions of the majority ... on the various items of applotment, in
> the way of amendments, regularly moved and seconded, we, the majority
> of the parishioners present ... protest against the proceedings of said
> vestry, and declare ... entire proceedings ... are illegal, and that we are
> not bound to comply in the way of assessment ...[36]

The value of this description of a vestry meeting is that it points to the anom-
alies of the vestry system at the time, and the encroachment on its legal pow-
ers by an increasingly confident and articulate Catholic middle-class, frustrated
with the legal restrictions on their participation in this institution empowered
by law to impose taxes on ratepayers. It also highlights the part played by
Synnott who was conscious of the relative status of a ratepayer as well as of the
financial burden it imposed. The meeting also shows him as a leading member of the local Catholic middle-class seeking a share in the political status to
a large extent monopolised at the time by the Protestant class. Personalities
contributed to the controversy. The level of controversy and tension at the
vestry meetings was influenced by the strength of individual personalities.
Synnott, Brennan and Burke were the main protagonists on the Catholic side
in the above account. Although subject to the descriptive limitations of the
newspaper report we get an impression of Synnott as calm, controlled, confident and popular.

The physical limitations of the room also contributed to the confusion and
tension. The demands that the vestry meeting be adjourned to the local school
was as much a symbolic attempt to remove the meeting from Protestant control as a practical effort to find adequate space.

At a similar meeting in the parish about two years later, Synnott was joined
by other important local personalities.[37] These included James Bury, a supporter of the Repeal movement, who in 1840 won a seat on the reformed city
council, and who along with Synnott and Patrick Gardiner represented St.
Paul's electoral ward as Guardians of the North Dublin Union in 1839 and
1840.

The parish vestry was not the only forum for rising politicians like Synnott
at this time. The newspapers provide various snapshots of him playing a key
role at other meetings in the parish. In April 1839 his name appeared on a list
advertising a meeting of parishioners to address congratulations to Lord
Ebrington on his appointment as lord lieutenant.[38] In May of that year
Synnott was present at a meeting in Savage's Hotel chaired by James Bury
with Edward Brennan acting as secretary to prepare an address to the Queen
on the occasion of the so-called 'bedchamber plot.'[39] Synnott was one of eight
people appointed to form a committee to arrange a great meeting at which
support for the Queen could be expressed. This meeting took place some
days later at which Synnott proposed that

the firmness displayed by Her Majesty in repelling the offered insult in such an emergency, and on so trying an occasion, afford us additional proof (if any were wanting) of the fixed determination of her Majesty to uphold the prerogatives of the Crown ... [40]

This meeting was followed by an open air gathering on the 20 May near the new Catholic chapel in Arran Quay, which was attended by Daniel O'Connell and at which Synnott spoke.[41] A notice placed in the *Freeman's Journal* from about sixty of the burgesses of St Paul's ward in November 1841 to call a meeting at the local school room to promote Irish manufacture also included Synnott.[42] In 1843 the loss by the large local manufacturers, Purcell and Bourne, of the mail coach contract and its implication for local business and employment led Synnott to propose that a committee be formed to seek its restoration.[43]

Synnott along with other laymen clearly appears from these reports as a leading figure in St Paul's. Given the presence of so many articulate middle-class lay Catholics, Catholic clergy although present at some of these meetings did not appear to organise or control them.[44] These meetings reflected not a haphazard series of unrelated events, but an orchestrated expression of the policies and tactics of O'Connell's party. The support for the new lord lieu-tenant was an indication of the continuation of O'Connell's support for the Liberal administration. The references to the queen, besides displaying O'Connell's long-standing loyalty to the monarchy, were also an expression of satisfaction that the failed attempt of the prime minister, Robert Peel, to con-trol the appointment of the ladies of the queen's household had led to his res-ignation as prime minister. Many of these attitudes may well have been picked up at the repeal association meetings in Dublin and from reading the news-paper reports of them.

Synnott emerges as an important local figure in 1839 (there are few refer-ences to him in the contemporary newspapers before that year). By this time he had formed personal alliances with important local figures such as Patrick Gardiner (tobacconist) and James Bury (merchant), together with others like Edward Reilly (inn-keeper and vintner), Edward Brennan, James Burke, James Fallon, Patrick Lambert (baker) and Patrick Dunne (grocer). These men, all Catholics and most of them businessmen, represented rising Catholic middle-class power in the area in and near St Paul's.

SUPPORTER OF DANIEL O'CONNELL

The *Freeman's Journal* of 13 January 1842 includes Synnott among a list of the subscribers to the O'Connell tribute for 1841 at a meeting held in the new Catholic chapel in Arran quay. The list is arranged according to the subscription made and gives some indication of Synnott's social position among the middle-classes in the parish. At the top was Dr. William Yore the well known and popular parish priest of St Paul's Catholic parish, who contributed £10. He was followed by Patrick Gardiner (alderman) who contributed £5. James Fallon (town councillor) contributed £3. His name was followed by four men who contributed £2 each. These included Burke and Bury (both councillors). Political power appeared to parallel material wealth, although the publishing of lists such as this one might have exerted a degree of pressure on the subscribers to give more than their circumstances allowed. Synnott's name appeared in the middle of the list along with thirty-six others with a subscription of £1 each.

Contemporary newspapers are the only source found for Synnott's support for and involvement in the repeal association, founded by O'Connell in the 1840s to repeal the Act of Union of 1800 which united the Irish and British parliaments. Synnott's links with the association are also clear from front page notices of collections in St. Paul's parish. In one he is described as a repeal warden.[45] O'Connell's instructions to repeal wardens were published in a small 12 page booklet of 1843.[46] They show the political and organisational skills of O'Connell in raising money and in promoting the association at local level. A warden had to possess an intimate knowledge of his district, be able to articulate the arguments in favour of repeal and promote the registration of electors, corporation and boards of guardians of the poor law unions. We know here what might have been expected of people like Synnott and presumably what others saw in him. A review of the detailed reports of the repeal association in the more nationalist newspapers reveal no mention of Synnott, which suggests that he did not rise above the rank of warden. However, what is emerging by the mid-1840s is a person of some local stature.

SYNNOTT AND THE NORTH DUBLIN UNION

The Irish poor law system was established in 1838.[47] The country was divided into 130 unions which were themselves divided into electoral divisions, each of which returned elected and ex-officio representatives. The ex-officio members were from the local magistracy, and most were members of the Established church. In the North and South Dublin unions, the predominance of Protestant ex-officio members (twenty-one out of twenty-two) is striking though not unusual.[48] Protestant and property interests were strengthened further in 1843 when the proportion of ex-officio guardians was increased from 1:3 to 1:2.[49] This conservative and Protestant influence on the boards of guardians is important for understanding the political and religious context in which Synnott found himself as a member of the board of the Dublin North Union. Many of the controversial issues at these meetings had sectarian or political undertones which often led to divisions along Catholic/Protestant lines.

The number of elected guardians in 1839 was thirty three for each of the city unions.[50] However the Protestant conservatives on the board (those which were elected, in addition to ex-officio) increased the numerical strength of that group.

The principle of local property being responsible for local poverty was at the heart of the system. Three-quarters of board members were elected by ratepayers. The voting system was weighted in favour of property owned or occupied. Government-appointed commissioners decided on the value of the property qualification necessary to be eligible to be a guardian. Synnott's eligibility as a guardian made him a member of an elite group.

The first election to the newly established poor law unions attracted much interest as is indicated in the extensive newspaper coverage of the time. Meetings of ratepayers, which were held in the wards of the city and county to select candidates, tended to be controversial, because they were often organised by one side or other of the political divide. Synnott, Gardiner and Bury were nominated at a meeting of some ratepayers in St Paul's, much to the dissatisfaction of local Protestants who had not attended what one of them called this 'hole and corner meeting'.[51] According to a church warden, Henry Price, those who selected them were not representative of the 'wealthy and respectable inhabitants'.[52] It would seem that the two words 'wealthy' and 'respectable', both having a similar meaning at the time, were in fact euphemisms for 'Protestant'. The accusations made at the vestry were later denied at a meeting of the ratepayers supporting Synnott, Gardiner and Bury. These latter three were described as honest, liberal, respectable and humane. In his brief election address Synnott accused Rev Lefanu and his party of being sectarian, citing as an example their refusal to allow the vestry to be used for a meeting to collect relief for the poor.[53] This remark about the use of the vestry contrasts with previous inclinations by Synnott's party not to use the vestry room for meetings. The hopes of some newspapers' correspondents that the election would be above party and creed had clearly not been realised in this parish, and Synnott, it appears, was also prepared to join in the political mud-slinging.

Table 1.2 shows the three victorious candidates, and the clear majority received by them. It indicates that Synnott had by now become a prominent and popular local figure on a par with Gardiner and Bury. The results also suggest the effectiveness of the O'Connell political machine, and the numer-

Table 1.2   Votes in St Paul's Ward for the Board of Guardians of the North Dublin Union, 1839

Patrick Gardiner	780	Jonathan Hardin	386
James Bury	743	William Courtney	357
Thomas L. Synnott	735	William Wynne	342

(Compiled from *Dublin Evening Mail*, 12 July 1839.)

ical superiority of the local Catholic middle-class. The three Catholic candidates had shared evenly between them 65 per cent of the votes cast.

In only four of the fourteen wards in the North Dublin union were the elections uncontested. All of the city wards were contested. It was in these wards
that the inhabitants were concentrated and meetings could more easily be
arranged to select candidates and organise support for them. Of the five uncontested wards in the South Dublin union, four were county wards.[54]

Table 1.3 North Dublin Union election 1839

City Wards	No. of Candidates	No. Elected	County Wards	No. of Candidates	No. Elected
Custom House	4	3	Clontarf	2	2
St. George	12	3	Howth	2	2
Post-Office	7	3	Cooloch	3	2
Linen-Hall	6	3	Glasnevin	6	2
Four Courts	9	3	Drumcondra	2	2
St. Paul's	6	3	Blanchardstown	1	1
			Castlenock	3	2
			Finglass	4	2

(Compiled from *Dublin Evening Mail*, 12 July 1839.)

As a member of this new institution in Ireland, and as one of those helping to
shape it, Synnott shared a unique experience with the other board members.
The interpretation and application of the laws concerning the structure of the
Irish Poor Laws on what was to become one of the busiest unions, rested to
some extent on the guardians. Other issues not accounted for in the law had
also to be considered. The minute books provide a rather impersonal and limited picture of what took place at these meetings, while the newspapers are
more expansive. For instance the conflict between the poor law commissioners and the North Dublin board over the pressure on the Dublin unions by
paupers sent from England prompted Synnott's description of the Commission
as 'useless lumber'.[55] There is also a graphic description of the reception of a
large number of paupers in 1840 when Synnott with some others was described as 'exceedingly active in selecting those whom they knew to be de-
serving in the wards which they represented.'[56]

Even the sparse minute books point to the huge burden placed on the
guardians. The board held weekly meetings. These varied in length, some of
the exceptional ones lasting up to five hours. It appears that some of the
guardians also attended at the workhouse on a second day of the week to assist in the admission of paupers. Synnott's record of attendance at the board
meetings was good. Out of twenty board meetings held between June and

November 1842, he was present at fifteen. Table 1.4 shows how this compares with a random selection of the other guardians.

Table 1.4 Attendance at twenty board meetings of the North Dublin Union, June-Nov 1842

Ex-officio Members	Meetings Attended	Elected Members	Meetings Attended
John Barlow	10	John Gray	19
Major Cottingham	19	Thomas Synnott	15
William Rathbourne	7	Arthur Baker	2
Hans Hamilton M.P.	4	Thomas Arkins	18
Captain Lindsey	20	Edwards Reilly	17
		Patrick McLean	15
		Henry Irvine	5
		John Dodd	12

(Compiled from *Morning Register*, June-November 1842.)

Synnott, Bury and Gardiner appear to have ensured that at least one of them was present at each board meeting. At least one of them was present at all of the meetings except two in the period between 23 September 1840 and 24 March 1841.[57] In 1841 Gardiner and Synnott were re-elected along with Patrick McLean.[58] Synnott was re-elected without contest in 1842,[59] probably owing to his established reputation. It may also have been due in part to a feeling in many wards that standing against Catholic/repeal candidates in wards with strong majorities was futile. It is interesting that Synnott at this time was described not as a grocer or vintner but as a gentleman. It appears that it was at this stage that he adopted the letter 'y' in the spelling of his surname. There is also another suggestion of an attempt by Synnott to reflect his increasing public status. In the 1848 and 1849 editions of Thom's *Dublin Directory* he is described as a solicitor.[60] His name, however, is not included in the Kings Inns Submission Papers[61] nor is he listed in Burtchaell's and Sadleir's printed register of graduates of Trinity College, Dublin.[62]

Most of the issues raised at board meetings had to do with money and religion. The principle upon which the poor law was based – that property was responsible for poverty – meant that any natural inclination to provide for the poor was tempered by its effect on the pocket of the ratepayer. The removal of paupers from England, the number (and the cost) of rate collectors in the union, the difficulty of collecting from every ratepayer because of houses not being properly numbered, and the dispute among the board members over whether the contribution of the rural part of the union was sufficient were issues which took up a lot of time in the early years. These preoccupations were

inspired by their implications for local taxes as much as by concern for the
welfare of the paupers. Synnott showed himself capable of making clear and
informed comments on the issues involved. He showed a detailed knowledge,
for instance, of local taxes, and was appointed to a number of committees
dealing with financial issues.[63]

The other major concern was religion. While money issues often led to
members crossing religious and political lines, the issue of religion was more
divisive. One particularly sensitive issue was proselytising. Synnott generally
adopted a pro-Catholic stance in these matters. There was often tension between the board and the commissioners, all of whom were English, in the
early years. Here Synnott constantly argued for more rights for the board and
fewer for the commissioners. For example he condemned the efforts of the
commissioners to appoint collectors of the grand jury cess as collectors of the
poor law tax[64] demanding that the board not the commissioners appoint the
collectors. Perhaps the most serious incident during Synnott's tenure of office
concerned a pauper, Martha McKeon, who converted from being a Protestant
to a Catholic. Such changes were frequent enough and generally acceptable
once the board was satisfied that no coercion had been used in the conver-
sion. What was different in this case was that McKeon was later made an un-
paid assistant to the workhouse schoolmistress. The commissioners, in order
to maintain 'unbiased freedom of religious opinion', refused to sanction the
appointment.[65] The dispute went on for three months, and for six weeks the
business of the union was suspended by the board apart from essential duties
such as the purchase of food for the inmates. The dispute ended when the
commissioners accepted the opinion of the attorney-general that the commissioners could only dismiss those in receipt of payment. The *Freeman's Journal*
caught the political nature of this dispute in its editorial on 27 December 1842
with the following heading: 'Defeat of the commissioners-restoration of
Martha McKeon'. Synnott supported the appointment of McKeon in the
many divisions reported in the newspapers, but contributed little to the various debates.

We must not however conclude from the McKeon case that such power
struggles were constant. Relations between members on the board were often
more complex as for example when Synnott along with other Catholic members supported a motion of thanks to assistant commissioner Hall who was
leaving the North Union board.[66]

While Synnott was an articulate member of the board, he was not one of
the most frequent speakers nor did he display the wit, sharpness of mind nor
the ebullience of someone like Thomas Arkins (tailor and corporation sword
bearer), described once as a political 'brawler',[67] who represented the Four
Courts ward. Synnott comes across as a close ally of Arkins, seconding many
of his proposals and being supported likewise by Arkins. Synnott's support in
St.Paul's remained high. He was elected to the board altogether three times,

not seeking re-election in 1843 following his appointment as high constable and billet master for Dublin corporation.[68] By then his reputation had gone beyond St. Paul's.

HIGH CONSTABLE AND BILLET MASTER

The position of high constable was one of the sinecures of the municipal council. It was essentially ceremonial but did carry prestige. There is a contemporary description of the duties of the high constable which show the benefits of the office to the holder, one being attendance at Buckingham Palace.[69] Ceremonial precedence at such gatherings was a sensitive issue for the holders of sinecures, leading sometimes to disputes among them.[70]

The 1840 Municipal Corporations Act led to the loss of Protestant control of the Dublin municipal council and the distribution of its sinecures. Synnott's appointment to the position of high constable in 1842 received much publicity at the time. It took place in the context of the successes of O'Connell and his supporters in the elections to the newly reformed municipal council in 1841. It was controversial because it was seen by many as jobbery and contrary to the promise alleged to have been made by O'Connell that he would never support such appointments.[71] The appointment of Synnott also meant the removal of the incumbent Thomas Mulholland who, the opposition argued, had a large family and depended on its income. It was claimed in the municipal council meeting that it was O'Connell who wanted Synnott as high constable. Nobody disputed this claim.[72] Newspapers on both sides of the political divide seemed to agree that it was O'Connell's wish, though they differed in the way they reported the appointment. The *Morning Register* which supported O'Connell, reported that O'Connell wanted to be surrounded by people 'in his confidence'.[73] The conservative *Dublin Evening Mail*, however, asserted that Mulholland was 'proscribed by the Corporate Dictator to make room for a creature of his own, a Mr. Sinnott (sic)...'.[74]

According to some Mulholland was dismissed not so much for the reasons O'Connell had given but because he had voted for the tory Gregory and not for O'Connell's supporter, Morpeth, in the recent by-election. The fact that Thomas Arkins appeared with Synnott in the office of the high constable on the day after Mulholland had voted for Gregory, when he introduced Synnott as the new high constable, would appear to support this view. There was a contest for the position of city marshall and for sword bearer, but it appears that no one wished to compete with Synnott for high constable. A Mr. Nolan of Dawson Street had withdrawn in deference to O'Connell's wishes.[75] (By contrast in 1848 when Synnott resigned the post, eight contested for it).[76] Synnott was formally proposed and seconded at the Council meeting by his supporters from St. Paul's, Bury and Gardiner.[77]

The question remains: why did O'Connell choose Synnott? It is very likely that O'Connell had formed a good impression of Synnott personally through contact at Repeal Association meetings, and indirectly through information from Bury, Gardiner and Arkins who were well known Dublin repeal figures. Synnott's early involvement in local parish and workhouse affairs had demonstrated two things: an articulate and intelligent local figure and someone capable of winning votes and the support of local power brokers. These personal qualities must have been communicated somehow to O'Connell. Synnott's probable Protestant antecedents might also have influenced O'Connell, who frequently stressed the liberal non-sectarian credentials of the repeal movement.[78] The complete ineffectiveness of those at the council meeting opposed to the O'Connellites to defeat or even delay the motion to appoint Synnott is clear from the vote. Councillor Fitzpatrick's and Alderman Joseph Boyce's motion to postpone the matter for six months was defeated by thirty-five to six votes.[79]

Synnott's ability to influence people and win support is also reflected in the fact that within weeks of his appointment to high constable and billet master, his salary was raised from £75 to £100.[80] In 1848, following his resignation from that post, the salary of the high constable was reduced within weeks to

Table 1.5   *Principal Officer Appointments by Dublin Municipal Council in 1847 (all Catholics)*

Name	Position	Salary
Thomas Reynolds	city marshall	£250
Thomas Arkins	sword bearer	£150
Thomas Synnott	high constable	£100
James Curran	mace bearer	£100
James Egan	auditor	£75
Francis Crump	rent collector	£100
James Dwyer	rent collector	£100
Anthony Parsley	rent collector	£100
John Barrett	rent collector	£100
Patrick Byrne	rent collector	£100
James Dennan	basin keeper	£20
Patrick Fanning	turncock	£41
David Simpson	turncock	£41
John Fanning	turncock	£41
	two water baillifs	£300

(Compiled from *Freeman's Journal*, 27 January 1847.)

the much lower figure of £10.[81] He also benefited materially from his political contacts. In 1844 he acquired the contract to supply coal to the city assembly house which earned him £42.[82] Table 1.5 shows how Synnott's salary and his relative influence as high constable compared with the other major municipal appointments. It also shows that important public positions for Catholics had increased dramatically since the municipal reform act of 1838. Synnott's increasing importance as an O'Connellite is also reflected in his selection in October 1843 by the secretary of the repeal association, Thomas Ray, to set out on the main road north to Drogheda to turn back the people travelling to the planned repeal 'monster' meeting at Clontarf which had been proclaimed by the Dublin authorities at the last moment. Synnott reported that word of the proclamation had reached Drogheda as late as nine o clock on the evening before the planned meeting.[83]

The years from the 1830s to 1848 marked a great change in the life and career of Synnott. His connection with the vintner/grocer class in Dublin and his subsequent (and consequent) rise in prominence as a vestry officer and local speaker at public meetings, place him in the classic middle-class Catholic repeal mould for that time. However while he did not attain election as a city councillor (there is no evidence that he sought it), his election as a workhouse guardian and as high constable had brought him to a political prominence reached by few of his repeal colleagues.

Synnott and Voluntary Famine
Relief 1845–50

Thomas Synnott played a major part in relief work during the great famine as secretary to various committees. In 1845, he was appointed secretary to the Mansion House relief committee. In 1846 he was secretary to the trustees of the Indian Relief Fund, and in December of that year he was appointed secretary to the more important General Central Relief Committee for all Ireland on the recommendation of the trustees of the Indian fund.[1] In his work with these committees, large sums passed through Synnott's hands. His role in the distribution of the large sum of £98,000 emphasises the important part he played in the famine. We know from the reports of these committees[2] that it involved the keeping of accounts, the forwarding of application forms to those who sought relief and the collating of their responses. We are less clear about his involvement in the decisions about how and where the aid was to be distributed. He does not appear to have worked simultaneously with these committees. Once the main function of one had been accomplished, he was appointed to another on the recommendation of the previous one.[3]

The amounts distributed by other important voluntary committees in Table 2.1 below indicates the relative importance of Synnott's work in the famine.

Table 2.1 Major voluntary committees in Ireland 1845–50[4]

Name of relief committee	Amount
Indian Relief Fund	£14,000
Central Relief Committee	£84,000
Irish Relief Association	£42,000
Society of Friends Committee	£200,000
Ladies' Relief Association	£20,000
British Relief Association	£391,701

Note: The Central Relief Committee should not be confused with the Central Relief Committee of the Society of Friends in this study. When reference is being to the latter, it will be clearly indicated as such.

Synnott was also closely involved with Daniel Murray, the Catholic archbishop of Dublin, in the distribution of a large amount of relief sent to the archbishop from around the world, most of it in 1847.[5]

MANSION HOUSE COMMITTEE

The Mansion House Committee was set up in 1845 to enquire into the extent of the potato blight. Its function was to obtain accurate statistical information from local civil and religious leaders throughout the country. Synnott's appointment as secretary to this committee was due in part to the prominence he had achieved in Dublin over the previous six years. Other qualities such as accounting skills, perhaps inherited from his father and developed as a grocer, must have influenced those who selected him. The strong 'repeal' profile of the committee would also have helped. The members of the twenty-six-member committee all knew of him in his role as high constable and many of them such as Patrick Gardiner, William Yore, Thomas Bermingham, and Daniel O'Connell knew him personally over a longer period. The qualities of integrity, zeal, and 'a great facility in transacting public business'[6] attributed to him for his work with this committee must have been to some extent evident even before his appointment.

In his role as secretary, Synnott sent questionnaires to all Catholic and Protestant clergymen in Ireland, as well as justices of the peace and poor law boards. He collated their responses when returned.[7] Although the importance of this committee was offset by the positive relief quickly taken by the then prime minister, Sir Robert Peel, the committee did help to counter the arguments of some sections of the press in Ireland and England that there was no real crisis.[8] Such accusations prompted the committee to direct Synnott to prepare an analysis of 500 replies received which demonstrated that, although the potato crop was above average, about a third had been destroyed.[9] Table 2.2 below demonstrates the wide representation across the religious and political divide in the completed questionnaires received by Synnott. It also reflects his first of a number of widespread contacts in Ireland concerning the famine. Very likely many of those contacted here, especially Catholic clergy, maintained contact with him as secretary of later relief committees. It also indicates the felt need by this rather 'repeal' controlled committee to demonstrate its impartial credentials.

Table 2.2 Completed Questionnaires returned to Synnott as secretary to Mansion House Committee 1845

Denomination of sender	Total
Est. Church clergy	197
Catholic clergy	143
Presbyterian clergy	30
Deputy-lieut. + magistrates	107
Poor law guardians	23

(Compiled from *Dublin Evening Post.*, 2 Dec 1845)

The *Freeman's Journal* praised Synnott's report as having been carried out with 'great diligence, ability and a necessarily great expenditure of time and labour'.[10] Not all agreed with this. The conservative newspaper, the *Evening Packet*, criticised Synnott's analysis, claiming that the Mansion House Committee had created panic for 'factional purposes'.[11] Potato blight reports had become part of the political currency of the time. Further press criticism led to the circularisation of a second questionnaire. These new figures confirmed the earlier reports of a serious loss, and corroborated the government's own findings.[12]

The Mansion House committee does not appear to have had any further role in 1845 other than the collection and analysis of data on the blight, although the *Freeman's Journal* reported that some famine-stricken localities expected relief from it.[13] It did however help to broadcast warnings of the impending crisis at a time when other voices were creating doubt.[14] Synnott's work with the committee appears to have established him as a key figure in relief work. In addition to the praise received from some sections of the press, O'Connell, in a parliamentary speech, praised the 'minuteness and care' of Synnott's reports.[15] In a later personal reference in Synnott's favour which he sent to the lord lieutenant in July 1846, O'Connell was more fulsome:

> I can venture to assure your Excellency, which I do with the utmost sincerity, and after long experience, that it would be impossible for the Government to appoint a gentlemen better qualified than Mr. Synnott, in the approaching ... distress or rather famine ... [16]

Allowing for a possible element of exaggerated praise for a loyal repeal supporter, these words, based on O'Connell's first-hand experience of Synnott's work, have an air of conviction about them.

SYNNOTT AND THE INDIAN RELIEF FUND

The work of the Mansion House Committee attracted the attention of people far from Ireland. In the spring of 1846 the inhabitants of Calcutta in India lodged £3000 for famine relief to its credit.[17] Synnott's widely praised work with the Mansion House Committee led to his appointment as secretary to the Indian Relief Fund set up in January 1846 to raise money for the relief of famine victims in Ireland. The fund, the first voluntary fund-raising committee in this famine, had its origins in Calcutta where news of the famine prompted the sheriff there to call a meeting of its inhabitants to raise funds for the Irish. The presence of the British army there, which included Irishmen in their ranks, must have played a part in inspiring the meeting. Between January and December of that year almost £14,000 was raised and forwarded to a pre-selected committee of leading and respected Irishmen in Dublin. Although all politically moderate, these trustees consisted of five Catholics and five Protestants,[18] indicating a concern (typical of many voluntary committees[19]) to be seen to be impartial. This concern is evident in the reluctance of some of the committee to meet for the first time without all ten of them being present.[20] Unlike the Mansion House Committee there was no clear 'repeal' element among the trustees, which indicates that Synnott's abilities were being recognised beyond his political milieu. In fact his position as secretary of this committee isolated him ideologically from the kind of political stance he might have adopted in earlier years. The trustees appear to have been sensitive to the possibility of its records being used for political purposes and were not as willing as the more nationalist Mansion House Committee to release the details of its relief work to the press. In June 1846 the *Freeman's Journal* questioned the wisdom and motives of the trustees in refusing to permit any portion of their correspondence to be published. The newspaper had approached Synnott for access to information which it believed might provide important statistical information. The Indian Relief Committee refused. The newspaper's editor, John Gray, felt certain that this decision could not have been unanimous.[21] Was this feeling based on information from Synnott who through his experience on the Mansion House Committee believed in the value of published famine statistics? Synnott also had worked with Gray on the board of guardians of the North Dublin Union, and both shared in common a support for O'Connell.

From the Dublin town house of its chairman, the duke of Leinster, the Indian Relief Committee arranged the distribution of their fund to some 830 parishes in almost every county in Ireland, the average payment being £30.[22] None of the Dublin parishes received aid from this fund,[23] a striking omission considering that the committee meetings took place in that city and that the trustees were therefore aware of the effects of the famine there. Again Synnott was responsible for the forwarding of questionnaires to applicants seeking aid, and the collating of the responses. Although the surviving evidence does not provide a clear picture of Synnott's role if any in deciding how the money was to be distributed, it is likely that it was important considering that he was the person directly in contact with the hundreds of applicants, and the one most familiar with the statistics contained in the completed questionnaires which were returned to the committee.

It was decided that relief would be given to areas which had not received aid from other sources, and then only after a minute enquiry into the state of each district requesting help.[24] As table 2.3 shows, a total of 520 local recipients received aid from the Indian Relief Fund for distribution in about 830 parishes (about 47 per cent of the parishes in Ireland). The average payment of £30 was a considerable figure if one accepts a contemporary belief that 2s. 6d. was sufficient to keep a family of five alive for a week, with such meagre recipes as a pottage of Indian meal, nettles, wild turnips and other herbs.[25] On the basis of this estimate £30 would have kept 1,200 persons alive for a week. The total amount collected by the end of 1846, £14,000, would have therefore been sufficient to feed 560,000, a large number by any standard, but for only one week. However according to Synnott's report, the total destitute in those districts who sent returns to him by December 1846 was 1,159,842. This fund's ability therefore to cater for the distress in Ireland in 1846 was very limited.

Some of the recipients applied a number of times. The committee reported 2,000 applications, only twenty of which were turned down. Therefore the religious and civil profile of the recipients may reflect both an attempt by the committee to be impartial and an expectation by the applicants that it would be so.

Table 2.3 Local recipients of aid from the Indian relief fund.

Province	R. C. clergy	Est. Church clergy	Magistrates etc.	Total
Leinster	19 (28%)	20 (33%)	29 (43%)	68
Ulster	33 (54%)	24 (39%)	4 (7%)	61
Munster	43 (21%)	80 (38%)	86 (41%)	209
Connacht	125 (69%)	20 (11%)	37 (20%)	182
Total	220	144	156	520

(Compiled from *Indian relief report*. The percentage referred to above is of the total recipients for each province)

Other religious denominations, such as the Presbyterian and Methodist, were not included among the named applicants, but they may have been members of the local committees through which much of this fund was distributed.[26]

The differences in the civil and religious distribution of the recipients (Table 2.3) may have been less striking in cases where the Indian relief was distributed through local committees, because in such cases they were not the sole arbiters of where the money went, but the question remains: why did Catholic clergy account for 69 percent of the recipients in Connacht, and Protestant clergy account for 38 percent (compared to 21 percent for Catholic clergy) of the recipients in Munster? The large percentage of Catholic recipients in Connacht may indicate that they were the closest, and often the only, articulate source of intelligence concerning the distress of the largely Catholic population there. The strong representation of Protestants in Munster may be explained by the possibly greater number of Protestant clergy and gentry there.

A comparison between the grants made by certain voluntary relief committees reveals that the more Protestant ones (italicised in Table 2.4) gave a greater percentage of their funds to Munster than to Connacht. Was there a connection between the relatively large grants given to Munster by these Protestant committees and the fact that the greater proportion of Protestant recipients of the Indian Relief Fund were in Munster?

Table 2.4   Comparison between the percentage grants of certain committees to Munster and Connacht

Committee	% to Munster	% to Connacht	Total Grants
Indian Relief Fund	39	41	£13,920
Central Relief Committee	22	32	£78,024
Royal Exchange Committee	19	76	£5,326
Irish Relief Association	30	17	£38,415
Ladies' Relief Association	47	23	£13,571

(Compiled from the committees' reports. Those italicised were more Protestant in composition.)

Synnott's analysis at county level shows a fairly close relation between destitution and the relief given by the Indian fund. The percentage of aid ranged from 2.5 per cent for Wicklow to 0.04 per cent for Louth, the average being between 1 per cent and 1.4 per cent. (Table 2.5 shows the destitute numbers in descending order.).

Table 2.5 Relief by county. Indian Relief fund, 1846

Leinster	Destitute	Aid Given	Aid as % of Destitute
Kilkenny	27,119	£255	0.90
King's	18,404	£367	2
Meath	16,520	£275	1.70
Longford	15,529	£155	1
Wexford	11,759	£105	0.90
Westmeath	7,607	£25	0.30
Carlow	6,115	£72	1.2
Queen's	4,000	£30	0.80
Wicklow	1,400	£35	2.50
Louth	440	£15	0.04
Total	108,893	£1,434	1.30

Table 2.5 Relief by county. Indian Relief fund, 1846 (Contd.)

Ulster	Destitute	Aid Given	Aid as % of Destitute
Donegal	70,219	£588	0.80
Armagh	25,122	£305	1.20
Cavan	17,289	£265	1.50
Antrim	2,000	£50	1.30
Monaghan	2,000	£25	1.30
Down	950	£20	2
Fermanagh	800	£5	0.60
Total	118,380	£1,258	1

Munster	Destitute	Aid Given	Aid as % of Destitute
Cork	191,225	£1,587	0.80
Tipperary	103,995	£1,280	1.30
Clare	94,857	£1,260	1.30
Limerick	69,216	£645	0.90
Waterford	47,699	£460	1
Kerry	33,200	£185	0.60
Total	540,192	£5,417	1

Connacht	Destitute	Aid Given	Aid as % of Destitute
Mayo	163,420	£2,040	1.20
Galway	137,671	£2,860	2
Leitrim	32,500	£95	0.30
Sligo	30,132	£400	1.30
Roscommon	28,654	£235	0.80
Total	392,377	£5,630	1.40

Compiled from *Indian Relief* report, p. 21.

However a study for example of those parishes returned as having had exactly 2,000 destitute (presumably an approximation) shows that numbers of destitute sometimes had little relation to the relief awarded. Table 2.6 indicates the awards as ranging from £80 down to £10 (the award as a percentage of destitute ranging from 4 per cent to 0.5 per cent).

Table 2.6 Parishes with 2,000 Destitute

County	Parish	Grant	Grant as % of Destitute
Mayo	Kilmolara	£80	4
	Ballintubber	£80	4
	Partry	£60	3
	Kiilasser	£50	2.5
	Meelick	£45	2.25
	Kilfian	£40	2
	Killalla	£15	0.75
Galway	Ahascragh	£70	3.5
	Oranmore	£60	3
	Spiddal	£60	3
	Ballymacaward	£45	2.25
	Moycullen	£20	1
	Adragoole	£15	0.75
Donegal	Killybegs	£47	2.35
	Garton	£36	1.8
	Raphoe	£25	1.25
	Glen Columbkill	£15	0.75
Clare	Killone	£40	2
	O'Brien's Bridge	£40	2
	Clondagad	£25	1.25
	Kilfiddan	£25	1.25
Tipperary	Tipperary	£50	2.25
	Ikerrin	£40	2
	Knockerilla	£25	1.25
	Drangan	£15	0.75
King's	Egish	£12	0.6
	Phillipstown	£10	0.5
	Frankford	£10	0.5

(Compiled from the *Indian relief report*)

The disparity in the above table may indicate other criteria being used in addition to destitution for deciding on relief. The questionnaire required to be

completed by applicants sought information not only on the total destitute,
but also on the extent of public works in the district and average wage given,
local price of meal and bread, the amount of the local subscription to relief,
the availability of seeds for the coming spring and the number of deaths from
starvation.[27] Distribution of relief by Synnott and the committee depended to
a large extent on the reliability of local intelligence (unlike the committee of
the Society of Friends which had its own experts in various areas to ascertain
the extent of destitution).[28] It may also have depended on the reputation or
influence of the individual applicants. There is a close link at parish level between relief and deaths from starvation, which suggests that this may have
been an important consideration in the minds of Synnott and the committee.
Synnott's questionnaire sought details on the number of deaths from starvation. The relief given shows an obvious link with such deaths. Parishes recording thirteen or more deaths by starvation are included in the following
sample. The deaths are presented in descending order.

Table 2.7 Parishes with 13 or more deaths from starvation

County	Parish	deaths/ starvation	Relief	Destitute
Clare	Kilmurry+eleven others	60	£40	7,000
Clare	Kilfarboy	25	£25	4,500
Cork	Kilcashen+two others	20	£30	3,500
Clare	Kilfearagh+Killard	20	£30	4,000
Galway	Ballindereen	18	£15	1,500
Mayo	Kilcommon West	15	£10	5,000
Galway	Kilcooney	13	£15	3,000
Mayo	Killedan +Kiltimach	13	£10	700

Compiled from *Indian Relief report*, pp. 7–21.

It is impossible to be exact about the degree to which distribution of this fund
related to destitution and deaths by starvation, but there was a clear effort by
the committee to distribute according to perceived need. It also appears that
when distributing relief the committee, and presumably Synnott, were more
attentive to large areas such as counties. When sending relief to local community leaders they were not so much concerned about the extent of destitution
in the immediate localities of the recipients, provided it also found its way to
the destitute in the wider area. Deaths by starvation (often in practice difficult
to separate from deaths from disease) was an emotive enough description to
merit special mention in the newspapers, and probably prompted special consideration in the distributing of aid.

There is very little detail recorded on the administrative expenses incurred by this fund. We know simply that £180 was spent on expenses such as 'salaries, advertising, postage, printing, stationery, etc.' However it is also known that the total fund of £13,919 was distributed at 1 per cent cost,[29] a small percentage if compared with other relief committees. This achievement must have been due in part to Synnott's efficient management of the correspondence and of the clerical work of the trustees. The expenses of the Central Relief Committee (2.3 per cent) of which Synnott was secretary from the end of 1846, also reflects his management ability. Table 2.8 below shows how its expenses compare with certain other national voluntary committees.

Table 2.8 Expenses of certain Voluntary Committees

Committee	Date	Expenses (% of total)
Indian Relief Fund	Apr.–Dec. 1846	1
Central Relief Committee	Jan.–Dec. 1847	2.30
Irish Relief Association	Sept. 1846–Aug. 1847	8.20
Ladies' Relief Association	Jan.–Sept. 1847	2.40
Royal Exchange Relief Committee	May.–Sept. 1849	2

Compiled from the printed reports of these committees. (Those italicised employed Synnott as secretary)

The Dublin liberal newspapers heaped praise on Synnott for his work with the Indian fund. His report for the fund ' had long ago found its way into the hands of every subscriber at Calcutta, and we doubt not that they will readily admit that a more lucid and satisfactory statement of financial affairs has never been submitted to a charitable society'.[30] Such praise, some of which came from English newspapers,[31] supports other evidence that Synnott was a main contributor to a well-organised and efficiently-run committee, as well as an example to later committees.

SYNNOTT AND THE CENTRAL RELIEF COMMITTEE

The Central Relief Committee was set up in December 1846 following disagreement among leading Dublin men about whether a committee for Dublin's destitute poor, or one for the whole country, should be established. The outcome was the establishment within days of two committees exclusive of each other. Rev Andrew O'Connell, parish priest of St. Michael's and

John's, was the main mover behind the Metropolitan Relief Committee which was intended to co-ordinate the activities of Dublin parish-based committees.[32] The fact that the Central Relief Committee was founded so soon afterwards suggests that its intention from the start was to relieve only areas outside Dublin. Synnott was invited to become its assistant-secretary on the recommendation of the Indian Relief trustees. This was a much larger committee with forty-five members which included the experience of three from the Indian Relief Fund and five from the Mansion House Committee. Synnott was one of only a small number with experience in both of these committees. These included Daniel O'Connell and Daniel Murray, the Catholic archbishop of Dublin.[33] The profile of this committee again suggests an effort to be above party politics and to be seen to be so. However the praise for the work of the landed class in famine relief in their report for December 1847 reflected its rather Protestant upper and middle-class though liberal ethos in contrast for instance to the more Catholic Royal Exchange Committee which tended to be critical of the landed class.[34] Murray's membership on the Central Relief Committee must however not be underestimated. A large portion of the funds received by it came through him. Again Synnott's selection as secretary reflected a widely-held recognition of his ability. Murray's confidence in this committee, unusual for a member of the Catholic hierarchy, was based on his belief that multi-denominational committees should be supported by the hierarchy. It was also due to his respect for Synnott.[35]

As with other committees the Central Relief Committee emphasised a determination to help only those in greatest need. To ensure impartiality the relief for several months was distributed chiefly to local committees rather than individuals. In 1849 it was decided to distribute it mainly through Catholic clergy because they were the only applicants at that time. Even then all the local clergy were notified and their cooperation sought and apparently in most cases received in the distribution of relief.[36]

Although there was cooperation among the voluntary committees, and between them and the government agencies, there was also tension, as for example between the Central Relief Committee and the Royal Exchange Committee. The latter committee was established in 1849 in Dublin by Fr John Spratt, the well-known Carmelite priest. Both committees cooperated at the beginning by exchanging data. However the tension between them was clear in a letter from Lord Cloncurry in which he reflected that 'one set is for aiding the Pope ... the other's for aiding the landlords and not the tenants'.[37] Cloncurry was a member of the Central Relief Committee and though he and Spratt respected each other, he was reluctant to allow his name to be publicly linked with the Royal Exchange Committee. Relations were further soured when the Central Relief Committee refused to cooperate with the Exchange Committee's proposed visit to England to raise more money.[38] While there the deputation discovered that their contacts there had been fed with descriptions of their committee as a 'popish and priestly concern'.[39] Therefore we find Synnott here linked to a committee some members of which were very probably involved in disseminating such sectarian language. It is also interesting that Murray in spite of such antagonism against 'Catholic' committees, remained a supporter of the Central Relief Committee. Other complex factors sometimes blurred the political and religious polarisation of that time. While they would have clearly dissociated themselves from such language, Murray and probably Synnott shared a liberal attitude in their dealings with non-Catholics and found their committee generally tolerant and impartial in the distribution of relief.

The Central Relief Committee distributed the large sum of £84,000 between January 1847 and May 1849.[40] In money terms it ranked third behind the committee of the Society of Friends and the less-profiled British Relief Association. Most (some £60,000) of the Central Relief Committee's aid was given in 1847.[41] As with the Indian Relief fund, Dublin was not considered as a focus of aid, receiving only £30. However the committee did provide £400 to the lord mayor to relieve paupers being forcibly returned from England.[42] A request for additional aid for this purpose led to a meeting in 1847 between the committee and the lord mayor.[43] This it seems was an exceptional move necessary for relief to be given to Dublin. Subsequent to this meeting a further £410 was given. A trip by Synnott to Liverpool on behalf of the committee which took place sometime between July 1848 and May 1849[44] may have been arranged to ascertain the extent of the problem of the removal of paupers from England, most of whom travelled through Liverpool and many of whom eventually arrived in Dublin seeking relief at its two city workhouses.[45] Such aid for Dublin appears to have been exceptional. Table 2.9 suggests that some relief committees considered that Dublin and other large towns had other resources to deal with their own destitution. On behalf of the Central Relief Committee, Synnott received returns from only two Dublin parishes while the more distant Kilkenny and Wexford returned twenty-one and thirty-eight parishes respectively.[46] Therefore it would appear that Dublin relief workers did not send returns because they did not expect funds from the Central Relief Committee. Perhaps Synnott, given his strong local ties, was of a like mind with the widely-held view of voluntary committees that large cities should take care of their own destitute poor.[47] If he felt that the committee should help Dublin then he was in a better position than most to know, or find out, the state of destitution in the Dublin parishes. Table 2.9 shows the amount given to Dublin by a number of voluntary committees.

Table 2.9 Relief Given to Dublin City and County by certain Voluntary Committees

Committee	Amount given to Dublin	Total fund	%
Indian Relief Fund		£13,919	
Central Relief Committee	£840	£84,000	1
Irish Relief Association	£20	£38,415	0.05
Ladies' Relief Association	£891	£20,159	4.4
Royal Exchange Committee		£5,326	
Total	£1,751	£161,819	2.8

Calculated from the printed reports of the above relief committees.

It is quite startling for instance that, while Dublin people contributed £2,884 of the total of £5,484 collected by the Royal Exchange Committee, none of it went to relieve Dublin's destitute poor. [48]

Again while Synnott's official duties as secretary are clear from the reports of the Central Relief Committee, the extent of his influence has to be surmised. Synnott once again received great praise for the 'great ability and care with which he has managed the accounts'. He dealt with about 70,000 items and according to the auditors every payment and receipt was 'exactly' recorded and balanced.[49] He was thanked for providing his 'valuable assistance' gratuitously in 1849.[50] Such acknowledgements were not, it appears, written as a matter of form. In few of the reports of other committees viewed for this study was there any reported praise for their secretaries and in none is the praise for a secretary so effusive. Again given his accumulated knowledge of famine statistics and his repeated personal contacts with hundreds of leaders of distressed communities one must conclude that his influence went beyond the keeping of accounts and the preparing of statistics. Few members of the committee would have attended all the weekly meetings and some perhaps were not present at any. The excellent attendance of one of its members, Thomas Hutton, was noted by the newspapers. This implies that there were others who did not attend as often.[51] Synnott's influence here was determined by the nature of his work which required frequent attendance. He had to be present to deal with donations to the committee from around the world and with the forwarding of aid to destitute parishes. Even when subscriptions to the committee had dried up as they did during February 1847,[52] he had to deal with continuous begging letters, the preparation of accounts and the collating of returned questionnaires.

Throughout this period Synnott's 'diligence, business-like habits and high moral character'[53] were also noticed by Daniel Murray, the Catholic archbishop of Dublin. Murray had known him as a member of the Indian Relief Fund and the General Relief Committee, and while his commitment to the idea of working through multi-denominational committees was a matter of policy for him,[54] he must also have been encouraged by his personal confidence in Synnott. As the Murray papers in the Dublin Diocesan Archives indicate, there was in 1847 and 1848 a close collaboration between the two men in the distribution of famine relief.

SYNNOTT AND THE MURRAY FUND

In the Dublin Diocesan Archives there are some 400 manuscript letters, receipts and other documents which in part or in whole make reference to the great famine.[55] These are listed under the heading 'Murray papers' and can be broadly categorised in the following way: first there are letters sent to Daniel Murray, mainly from outside Ireland which refer to relief being sent to relieve famine victims and secondly there are letters received by Murray or Synnott from distressed parishes mostly in the west of Ireland acknowledging the receipt of aid and/or seeking (more) aid. These letters are an important and, up to recently, neglected source for a study of voluntary relief during this famine. In particular they provide an insight into the relief work organised by the Catholic church at international and local level, and especially Murray's role in its collection and distribution. Murray had worked with many charities before the onset of the great famine.[56] He was known for his membership of a number of voluntary committees through the contemporary newspapers, at a time when publicity was considered necessary to account for monies raised and distributed. However Murray did not appear to apply this policy of publicity to aid distributed by him, his fear being that it might generate expectations which he would not be able to meet.[57] This might explain the absence of external references to the Murray fund which according to a recent study was considered to have amounted to more than £60,000.[58] It might also explain why Murray never set up his own relief committee.

The Murray papers also highlight the collaboration between Murray and Synnott in the distribution of this 'Catholic' money. Almost eighty letters are addressed to Synnott. The recent discovery in the Dublin Diocesan archive of 118 receipts from the Central Relief Committee, signed by Synnott, for £5,551 given to it by Murray, makes clear the archbishop's support for this committee.[59] A printed list of subscribers to that committee also exists, and which includes some £12,000 contributed by Murray.[60] Allowing for monies accounted for in both of these sources the net total given by Murray was £16,086 which was just 20 per cent of the total fund of the Central Relief Committee. The total amount of relief sent to Murray, as recorded in the Murray papers, was £50,199 (this does not include 5,000 scudi received from Rome). There were

200 contributions, ranging from ten shillings to £6,633, the average amount being £243. Most of this money, which represents a considerable sum, was collected outside Ireland among Catholic congregations and individuals around the world, and nearly all of it in 1847. Most of the large sum for May of that year represents a collection made by the St.Vincent de Paul Society mostly in France. This society requested that their contribution be distributed in the following manner: 30 per cent to the archdiocese of Tuam, 40 per cent to the archdiocese of Cashel, and 30 per cent to be divided among six northern dioceses.[61] Dublin was not included.

Table 2.10 Relief sent to Murray each month in 1847, as recorded in the Murray papers.

Jan.	£8,311	July	£5,659
Feb.	£3,038	Aug.	£1,475
March	£3,241	Sept.	£2,920
Apr.	£2,537	Oct.	£1,637
May	£12,378	Nov.	£1,214
June	£649	Dec.	£550

Compiled from correspondence in the Murray papers.

Most of the money received by Murray was forwarded by him to other Irish bishops. Some of it was sent directly from the donors to local bishops, in some cases because of the donor's wishes (as was the case with the St.Vincent de Paul Society). But most of the donations were sent directly to Murray (92 per cent), perhaps an indication of the wide respect for him. However £13,336 of this was transferred by him to other Irish bishops. The incomplete nature of the Murray papers is evident in Table 2.11 which shows that a large portion of the money received by Murray is unaccounted for. Synnott is linked to a very small amount but this may not accurately reflect his full involvement with the Murray fund. Given the existence of the large number of receipts from the Central Relief Committee in this archive and the printed evidence elsewhere of other payments to this committee by Murray, it would seem likely that Synnott's involvement was greater than the figures show. The unaccounted amount below may hold the answer to the extent of his involvement here. Some of the acknowledgements sent to Synnott were addressed to 21 Queen St, or 36 College Green (headquarters of the Central Relief Committee) or to his address at Grangegorman Lane, Dublin. This confusion about addresses may explain why so many acknowledgements did not find their way to the safe-keeping of the Dublin Diocesan Archives.

Table 2.11 Famine relief referred to in the Murray Papers

Amount received by Murray		£50,199
Amount forwarded by Murray *to other bishops*	£13,336	
Amount sent directly *to parish clergy* by Murray or Synnott	£976	
Amount given by Murray *to the Central Relief committee*	£11,922	
Total distributed by Murray, the destination of which is known		£26,234
Money received by Murray which *is not accounted for*		£23,965
Amount sent *directly (not through Murray)* *to other bishops*	£3,752	

Compiled from the correspondence in the Murray papers. (Amounts calculated upwards to nearest £).

The multi-faceted approach to the distribution of this relief, as indicated in these figures, reflected disagreements among the Irish Bishops about methods of distributing the 'Catholic' relief. Murray preferred to work through 'mixed committees' (i.e. multi-denominational committees). In a letter to Michael Slattery, the Catholic archbishop of Cashel, in February 1847, he appeared to be in doubt as to how to distribute relief whether through the bishops or the Central Relief Committee.[62] However it is clear that he had by the end of January already made up his mind on the latter approach, having handed over to the committee through Synnott more than £3,000.[63] Among the four archbishops only Crolly of Armagh agreed with Murray that Catholic relief should be distributed through 'mixed' committees. Murray it appears feared that a denominational approach to the distribution of relief might prevent the most destitute from receiving aid, as well as deepening the existing political and religious tensions.[64] Murray was however obliged by some of the donors to forward a share of the money received by him to the other archbishops.

The Murray letters provide a firsthand and a moving account of the effects of the famine on a number of parishes. The writers besides acknowledging money received from Murray go on to give a graphic picture of the suffering of their parishioners. One such writer was Fr Peter Ward parish priest of Partry in county Mayo who on 5 March 1849 wrote to Synnott acknowledging the receipt of £10:

> My Ever Dear Friend, I had been in chapel surrounded by at least seven
> hundreds of my poor parishioners praying for our benefactors, when your
> happy letter arrived. It is hard to describe their sensation as well as that of
> mine on the occasion. They, and I, were without one single penny ... [65]

The aid given by Murray and Synnott to the priests of distressed parishes was
in seventy-one separate payments and went directly to people who were more
aware than perhaps even the bishops of those most in need. The deep appreciation expressed by the recipient priests shows the high value they put on
what may appear today to be small sums such as £10 or £15. One can catch
in the above letter some sense of the suffering endured in such western
parishes and the widespread appreciation for and dependence upon Synnott.

Ward and the other recipient clergy were clearly aware that Murray was
the real source of much of much of the relief received (in forty-three of the
letters Synnott was asked to thank Murray), but the many references to the
Central Relief Committee show that the priests were aware that Synnott was
communicating with them as secretary of that committee. He was however
not considered a mere functionary. Some sent greetings to his family. One
congratulated him on his appointment as governor of Grangegorman prison.
Others such as William Flannelly of Clifden, county Galway, and Thomas Timlin
of Ballina, county Mayo sought and accepted his advice. Four of the letters
complained about the obligation to repay loans of money and seed provided.[66]
The priests may well have been referring to the Central Relief Committee
which made such arrangements and hoped that Synnott would intercede for
them to have such repayments waived. It is interesting that, while Synnott was
warmly acknowledged in many of the letters, no such feelings were expressed
for any other member of the Central Relief Committee, apart from Murray.

Synnott was very involved in the distribution of aid to the clergy in these distressed parishes. Fifty-six of a total of the seventy-four letters from priests in counties Mayo and Galway were addressed to him. These two counties received most
of the relief sent directly to priests (70 per cent). Mayo and Galway counties were
generally considered among the counties most affected by the famine. However,
the imperfect nature of the record may hide a possibly larger number of acknowledgements from these and other impoverished counties. The other counties for which there are acknowledgements are: Cork (ten letters acknowledging
£73); Tipperary (three acknowledging £10); Roscommon (two acknowledging
£30); Sligo (six acknowledging £50); Fermanagh (one acknowledging £15) and
Cavan (one acknowledging £40). 1848 was the busiest year for the Murray distribution to individual priests. Only a small number of letters were received
from the distressed parishes in 1847. This may have been due in part to the
existence of other voluntary groups, such as the Society of Friends, who were
active in that year. There was not the same sense of urgency as in 1848 and
1849 when famine still raged and voluntary relief was at a trickle.[67]

The correspondence in the Murray papers from other bishops makes little reference to Synnott. This is not surprising given that most of it dealt with money going directly, or through Murray, to them. However a letter from Synnott to Murray on 15 July 1848 suggests that Synnott was not simply passing on money received from Murray.

> The Bishop of Elphin called upon me with respect to the distribution of the £300 which I had the honor to receive from Your Grace and which I placed to your cr. in the Bank of Ireland when I told his Lordship that without an order from Your Grace I could do nothing in the matter, it was therefore my intention to have gone on this day to Maynooth and had an interview on the subject, but that I was told your Lordship would leave at an early hour for Tullamore. May I request your Grace will advise me how to act and what I am to do, pray dont *spare me* as perhaps there never was a moment when money was more wanting particularly in the *West* when the Landlords are ejecting in the most *inhuman* manner. His Lordship of Elphin is quite uneasy lest your Grace should imagine he was inclined to throw any trouble on your Grace, he also declines having anything to do with the *distribution* as he says it would create 'scruples in his breast', Your Lordship will please recollect this money cannot be drawn except by draft signed by your Grace.[68]

This letter raises a number of points which may help to throw light on Synnott's role in the distribution of the Murray fund. It shows that Synnott's collaboration with Murray extended beyond the management of relief set aside by Murray for the Central Relief Committee. At the time of the writing of this letter no decision had been made about how the £300 would be distributed. It does suggest therefore that Synnott was working not only for the committee but also for the archbishop. Even though this money was earmarked for the bishop of Elphin, Synnott showed himself to be anxious to assist Murray in its distribution even to the extent of travelling to Maynooth, a journey of some twelve miles from the offices of the Central Relief Committee at 36 College Green in Dublin from where he wrote this letter. The archbishop frequently made trips to Tullamore where he stayed at a friend's house in nearby Rahan.[69] Perhaps in these circumstances Synnott assumed a great deal of responsibility for the Murray fund, with the latter's permission and trust. Murray would also have depended on Synnott for details on the famine described by his clerical contacts in the letters sent to him. Moved by the destitution in western parishes and the cruelty of the landlords there as reported to him, Synnott in the above letter was quite strong in his recommendation about where the money should go. The bishop of Elphin's reluctance to have anything to do with the distribution was based on his belief that other parts of Connacht were in more need of it than his diocese.[70] In the conflict between the bishops over how the

Catholic money should be distributed, this bishop took Murray's side, leaving
its distribution to his discretion. Synnott therefore assumed the responsibility
on Murray's behalf for the distribution of the money. Synnott's willingness to
work unsparingly in relieving famine victims is acknowledged by many
priests, for instance in a letter from Martin Browne, parish priest of Balla, who
told him: 'your untiring exertions have contributed under Heaven to save the
lives of thousands'.[71]

The evidence points to the conclusion that Synnott played a major role in
voluntary relief during the famine. What the exact nature of that role was is
not always clear, but his accumulated experience and reputation must have
been a resource used by members of the committees for which he was secretary. Certainly his readiness to offer advice to Archbishop Murray and to
communicate information received from distressed areas suggests a pattern of
behaviour rather than isolated instances. Murray gave him responsibilities beyond that of a committee secretary, showing a great confidence in him. Synnott's
good reputation for secretarial efficiency, while it had its origins in the nationalist Mansion House Committee, was eventually recognised by a wider
community. The records are silent on his attitude to the question of whether
a national committee should relieve large towns like Dublin, but the failure
to locate any insight here suggests compliance if not support by Synnott with
the views of committees on this matter. The exact amount of money which
Synnott was involved in distributing is not known here but we do know that
it was more than £98,000. One source gives it as £180,000.[72] The difficulty
of ascertaining the exact amount is due to the incompleteness of the Murray
papers. What is perhaps clear is that his advice and sympathy, even his 'letter
listening', contributed to the moral support and physical relief of distressed
communities especially in parishes with no infrastructure to provide such help.

Although the difficulty of clearly ascertaining the full role played by Synnott
in famine relief remains, there appears little doubt that it was an important
one. By 1849 he had moved from being a local figure in St Paul's parish to
being a national figure to many communities around the country suffering
from famine. He was also by virtue of his involvement in relief committees
known to, and influencing and being influenced by, many of the wealthy and
powerful in Dublin business and political life. Synnott had by 1848 come a
long way from being the local shopkeeper of the mid-1830s.

Synnott and Grangegorman Female
Prison 1848–65

O n 12 May 1848 Synnott was appointed governor of the women's prison at Grangegorman.[1] The appointment was made on the assumption that a person who had excelled as secretary of the Central Relief Committee[2] would be capable of the responsibilities involved in prison management. The two jobs had some similarities, both involving the management of accounts and the preparation of statistics. However Synnott had no experience of the peculiarities of prison management in general, much less of those existing in Grangegorman. The duke of Leinster, chairman of the Indian Relief Committee, appeared to be aware of this when, in his recommendation to the lord lieutenant on Synnott's behalf, he added the following qualification that he considered Synnott no more than 'well worthy of consideration' for the office of governor and that 'unless he is found on enquiry to be perfectly qualified for that situation, I would not urge him on the notice of His excellency'.[3] Was the duke's hesitation based on some quality he observed in Synnott, in addition to his inexperience? The question is raised here because of certain events in his later years as governor which will be discussed below. The governorship was to bring him personal rewards, but also many difficulties, some of which were of his own making. Many of these achievements and problems were reflected in his relations with the most senior officers in the Irish prison service and are well documented in the existing government prison records. It is therefore possible to form a clearer picture of this part of his life. The political and religious tensions of the day which had found their own particular expression in prison life, ultimately contributed to his untimely departure from public life in 1865.

The foundation stone for the Richmond General penitentiary in Grangegorman was laid in 1812 and when completed, its imposing and forbidding frontage, surmounted by a central clock, measured almost 700 feet. A contemporary writer described it 'as calculated to produce in the mind of the approaching criminal an impression of hopeless incarceration'[4] (figure 5). For some of its destitute inhabitants that sense of foreboding was perhaps outweighed by the prospect of food and accommodation which the prison offered.[5] The drawings of the prison by Francis Johnston indicate that it was originally intended for male and female prisoners kept in separate sections,[6] but from 1836 it was used for women only.[7] The governor's apartments consisted of seven rooms at the front of the building, providing the Synnott family of four[8] surviving children with adequate accommodation. Over the years Synnott made

5. 'an impression of hopeless incarceration'. The former
Grangegorman Female Prison

improvements: a shower bath with hot and cold water pipes, a new marble
chimney piece, and in the prison grounds a large vegetable garden. In 1862
the board of superintendence provided him with a veranda over his hall door.[9]

There were two main classes of prisoner in Grangegorman from 1836. All
female convicts in Ireland who were sentenced to transportation spent three
months there, in that part of the prison known as the convict section, in preparation for their journey to the colonies. The other section of the prison – the
city section – was for the reception of all females under sentence of imprisonment in the city of Dublin. Table 3.1 below shows the number in these two
sections in Grangegorman on the day of the inspectors-general visit in 1848.

*Table 3.1   State of Grangegorman Prison on the 13 Feb 1848 showing totals of convict
and city inmates.*

Felons	85	Drunkards	<u>18</u>	
Receiving stolen goods	43	Total *of city prisoners*		442
Assault	14	Children of ditto.	<u>62</u>	
Breaking windows	10	Total of *Convicts*		209
Pawning illegally	4	Children of ditto.	<u>45</u>	
Selling spirits unlicensed	2	Total inhabitants		758
Misdemeanants	73			
Vagrants	132			
Lunatics	61			

Source: Twenty-seventh report on general state of prisons of Ireland, [1069] H.C. 1849 xxvi,
373, p. 34. The italicised words indicate the two main categories of prisoner.

The small number of drunkards (18 or 4 per cent of the city prisoners) is not an accurate reflection of the total for that year (see Table 3.3 below).

The city section of the jail was under the control of the nationalist Dublin municipal council. A board of superintendence visited the prison at least every fortnight. It was appointed by the council, to whom it submitted an annual report. Boards were appointed annually and selected from the members of the municipal council. Since they were chosen by lot they did not always reflect the distribution of power in the council.[10] The same board also visited the other city prison, the Richmond Bridewell, in the south of the city. Both prisons in 1858 were among the largest in the country, providing a proportionately greater status and salary for its senior officers (Table 3.2). The two prisons were closely linked administratively, both having the same local inspector and the accounts of both being kept at the Richmond.[11]

Table 3.2 *Jails with the largest daily average of prisoners in Ireland in 1858*

Grangegorman female prison	240
Richmond bridewell (for males)	230
Antrim	130
Cork	115
Tipperary, Clonmel	69
Tipperary, Nenagh	62

The remainder of the total of 42 jails had a daily average of less than 60.

Compiled from the *Thirty eight report on general state of prisons of Ireland*, [2691] H.C. 1860 xxxvi, 191, pp viii–ix.

There was a great reduction in the number of those committed to prisons in Ireland in the years after the great famine. However, Synnott's connection began at a time of expansion. A study of total numbers in Grangegorman in Table 3.3 reveals a greater number of prisoners in the years 1847 and 1848. This growth was mainly among the categories of drunkards and vagrants (30 per cent and 109 per cent respectively), possibly an effect of the famine on Dublin. The presence of lunatics, frequently referred to in the inspectors–general reports, seriously affected the level of discipline and general order.

Table 3.3 *Persons committed from the city of Dublin to Grangegorman in 1847 and 1848*

	1847	1848	%
Felons	328	310	−5
Misdemeanants	3,039	2,981	−2
Vagrants	609	1,274	+109
Drunkards	2,746	3,558	+30
Lunatics	50	60	+20
Total	6,772	8,183	

Source: *Twenty-seventh report on general state of prisons of Ireland*, [1069] H.C. 1849 xxvi, 373, p.34.

A comparative study of daily averages for the whole country in Table 3.4 shows the dramatic fall in numbers between the late 1840s and the late 1850s.

Table 3.4 Daily average of prison population for the whole of Ireland, 1847–50, and 1858–9

Year	Daily average
1847	8,900
1848	10,968
1849	12,648
1850	12,496
1858	2,894
1859	2,605

Compiled from the *27th., 29th. and 38th. reports on state of the prisons of Ireland.*

Besides the board of superintendence, two inspectors-general of prisons also visited the city section at least once a year on behalf of the government and presented an annual report to parliament. Inspectors were generally appointed from the Protestant and military class, the first Catholic among them being appointed in 1840.[12]

Their reports show their increasing dissatisfaction throughout the 1860s with the method of selection of the boards of superintendence: no account was taken of experience in the method of selection, and sometimes the political and religious representation was disproportionately Catholic and nationalist. In the 1860s such complaints were to be made in the context of doubts being raised about Synnott's efficiency and integrity.[13]

The other section of the prison – the convict section – was reserved for convicts awaiting transportation to the colonies and was directly controlled by the government through a single inspector. These prisoners, from every part of the country, spent three months in Grangegorman while being prepared for their new life in western Australia.[14] In 1854, in an effort to produce a more efficient prison service, the inspector of the convict section was replaced by a prisons board which comprised three inspectors.[15] This new board represented the establishment class, although one member, John Lentaigne, was a Catholic[16] (Lentaigne was later appointed one of the inspector-generals for the city section). The convict section of Grangegorman closed in 1859[17] when the last of the convicts there were removed to the new convict prison on the North Circular Road in Dublin, thereby reducing the responsibilities, the status and the salary of the Grangegorman officers, including Synnott. While the salary of the governor of the Richmond Bridewell remained at £400,[18] Synnott's was reduced from £300 to £200 when the convict section closed.[19]

Much of the information about Synnott's prison career is to be found in the printed reports of the inspectors-general. A careful reading of them sometimes points to tensions among prison staff, as for example between Synnott and the head matron, Marian Rawlins, in the report for 1849.[20] When Grangegorman had been reconstituted as a women's prison in 1836, Rawlins had been appointed as head matron there on the recommendation of Elizabeth Fry the prison reformer, who had known her for her work in Cold Bath Fields prison in London.[21] Rawlins was a formidable character, known and respected for the discipline and efficiency with which she approached the prisoners and prison organisation.[22] A Protestant, she had worked as nurse in the lord lieutenant's household.[23] It had been hoped, by Fry among others, that this prison for females would be run exclusively by females.[24] However, the prisons act of 1836 required that a woman could not be a keeper of such a prison as Grangegorman.[25] To comply with this legal requirement, a male governor was appointed and given responsibility for the stores, accounts, registries and books. The 'entire and uncontrolled'[26] management of the prisoners, an area in which Synnott had no experience, would remain under the direct control of an experienced matron. However the position of the male governor was rather insecurely based, more on a legal requirement than a felt need. The inspector-general who visited this prison in 1849, Nicholas Fitzsimons, recognised the difficulties which the governor had to face in this prison: while he was responsible for the safe custody of the prisoners and for the running of the prison, yet in practice he was not in a position to inspect it or make himself personally aware of how it was run. Fitzsimons, who noted the enthusiasm with which Synnott carried out his duties as governor, considered it absurd that the governor was so restricted, and recommended that Synnott should not only be authorised, but expected, to go through the prison at least once a day. There is a suggestion here that Fitzsimons was endeavouring to resolve a dispute between Synnott and Rawlins over perceived jurisdictions in the prison, and that he leaned towards Synnott in his efforts to resolve it.[27] The dispute however continued into the following year. The inspector-general who visited then, Frederic B. Long, suggested another remedy: Synnott would be relieved from all responsibility for the prisoners except in matters concerning their safe custody and in cases of riotous behaviour. He would superintend the male officers and be responsible for all the accounts and stores. As if to make it palatable to Synnott, Long suggested he might be allowed an assistant storekeeper. Rawlins, on the other hand, would have the entire management of the prisoners, though her duties would be 'strictly confined to this'.[28] She would no longer be in charge of the laundry account, which would now be the responsibility of the governor.[29] This rather even-handed proposal was, it appears, implemented,[30] but there is evidence in later years that the tension was never far beneath the surface. In any conflict over authority roles, Rawlins, who was well-established in her routines there since 1836, did not yield easily.

The tension between the governor and the female department was evident in a number of disputes. One of these, in 1862, concerned the Timmons family, when two of the senior matrons, Rawlins and Mary O'Carroll, the deputy matron, conspired to prevent Mr. Timmons from visiting his wife who was a prisoner there, in the face of Synnott's order that the visit be allowed. Synnott's anger, especially at O'Carroll, is evident in his letter to the board. He described the humiliation he felt at this display of disobedience in front of many of the officers:

> I the Governor of the prison in the presence of all the officials have to put up with the insult and indignity thus offered me or act with more determination and suspend the Deputy-matron for non-compliance with my order.[31]

The conflict over authority roles continued however, often to be compounded (as explained below) by religious tensions, especially during the time of Margaret Aylward's imprisonment there[32] Synnott's (unsuccessful) application for the position of governor of the new convict depot (Mountjoy prison) on 31 August 1849, only one year after his appointment to Grangegorman, suggests that he was not happy as governor of that prison.[33] However he settled into the job with the same energy shown in the relief committees, and according to the yearly reports of the inspectors-general, with a considerable degree of success. These reports are important because they show the inspectors-general to be very satisfied with Synnott's performance as governor up to 1861. The prison governors themselves sometimes influenced aspects of the reports, as for instance when Synnott complained to Henry Hitchins, the inspector-general of the convict section, that his name had been omitted from the report of the board of superintendence in 1850. Hitchins promised a favourable comment in his next report.[34] The reports generally appear to run to a formula. The inspectors-general had a busy countrywide annual schedule, and may therefore have sometimes made hurried inspections, although the Dublin prisons were more accessible than the country prisons to their office in Dublin Castle.[35] However, the comments on Synnott up to 1861 are often effusive and detailed in their praise, suggesting that some of the inspections were thorough.

The prison records of the 1850s depict Synnott as a hard working governor. Some of this information comes from Synnott himself.[36] But even people who were not his natural political allies made similar comments. One inspector (Corry Connellan) wrote in 1851: 'Mr. Synnott is a most zealous and conscientious officer'.[37] The well preserved governor's journals in Synnott's legible hand provide daily reports on life in Grangegorman prison. They are generally brief and repetitive but give an insight into the routine of prison life, the constant checks and the many written records which had to be made every day. No fewer than eighty-seven journals and account books were kept at Grangegorman in the 1850s. Nine of these were kept in the governor's office, and included the governor's journal, a register of juveniles sentenced to reformatories, a register of convicts sentenced to penal servitude, a stock ledger, an officer's leave of absence book and an officer's report book. Synnott was also ultimately responsible for the registers and ledgers kept by other male officers such as the registries of prisoners committed for trial, another for those on remand, one for drunkards, one for juveniles and one for vagrants. Altogether forty-five journals and ledgers were kept by the male officers.[38]

Synnott was also susceptible to the sorrows and joys of his family life. In June 1855 he sought a few days leave 'in consequence of his many family losses and being recommended relaxation from business by his medical officer'.[39] These losses included his wife, Marianne, who died in April of that year, aged thirty-seven years.[40] Synnott's family were not fully isolated from the more negative influences of prison life. In 1851 one of the prison staff, Charles Armstrong, threw a boot jack injuring one of Synnott's sons. His letter of apology to Synnott had a note attached to it by the inspector of prisons which points to a degree of kindness in Synnott: 'At Mr. Synnott's instance Armstrong is permitted to resume his duties as normal'. The inspector had intended suspending and transferring him to another prison.[41] In 1859 two of Synnott's sons earned the praise and a gratuity from the Board for the help they gave in putting out a fire in the prison. Synnott's report of the fire provides an interesting insight into the contemporary procedures for dealing with fires, and reflects, whether intended or not, his efficient handling of it.[42]

His personal income was important to Synnott judging by the number of pleas, one of which was jointly made with Rawlins, for an increase in salary.[43] He received £200 per year for his work with the city section of the prison, and in the early 1850s he received £40 for his work with the convict section. The latter salary was raised to £100 following a recommendation from Hitchins, the inspector of the convict section.[44] The salaries of some other public officials in Table 3.5 indicate the relative value of his income.

Table 3.5 Salaries of Grangegorman Prison Officers, 1849, city section

Governor	£200	Assist. Matron	£60
Clerk	£60	Store Matron	£40
Hall-door Keeper	£52	Other Matrons	£40 each
Guardsmen	£30	Other Matrons	£30 each
Head Matron	£200	Other Matron	£25
		Servants	£12 each

Compiled from *Twenty-seventh report on general state of prisons of Ireland*, H.C. 1849, [1069] xxvi 373, p.36.

Synnott, Rawlins and the deputy matron also received the following daily allowances: two pounds of bread, one quart of milk, four and a half stone of coal. They were also allowed one pound of candles and one pound of soap per week. These allowances were worth £98 in 1869.[45] Synnott therefore had a comfortable living relative to most other classes of prison officers, although much less so than those in more senior positions of authority. It is important to note here that although Synnott's salary was large in terms of the lower ranking officers, it would have been much higher had the authority structure, with its responsibilities divided between governor and head-matron, been different.

Table 3.6 Salaries of the members of the Government Prisons Board 1855

W. Croften	£700	rising to	£900
C.R. Knight	£600	rising to	£800
J. Lentaigne	£600	rising to	£800

(H. Hitchens' retirement allowance was £565)

Compiled from National Archives, Dublin, G.P.O. Carton 10, 1855.

Governors' salaries were not incremental and any increase seemed to depend on individual application and support from other more influential officers. The records of the 1860s suggest that Synnott's salary was not always sufficient to meet his standard of living. The city council's records reveal that in 1864 Synnott was required to attend a board meeting which intended to question him about an unsettled account with a retail firm in Dublin: his doctor reported that he was too ill to attend.[46] Following his dismissal in 1865 he was convicted as an insolvent debtor.[47] His creditors then spent a night in his prison apartments guarding his furniture in order to ensure repossession.[48] Synnott's concern for money was not unusual, but it is important to note it here because of the accusations and insinuations made against him in the 1860s.

The political tensions existing outside the prison between Conservative and Repealer, and between Protestant and Catholic, had implications for Synnott. Among the staff, Protestants greatly outnumbered Catholics in the 1840s, indicating Synnott's quite unique position as governor (Table 3.7). However, if one is to judge by the names of the Grangegorman staff in the 1850s and 1860s a greater proportion of Catholics were appointed then,[49] perhaps a sign that liberal governments were in office with whom Roman Catholics had good relations, and that there were improved education opportunities for middle-class Roman Catholics after the opening of the Queen's Colleges.

Table 3.7 Religious Denomination of prison staff in Grangegorman, April 1847

Protestant (Total:20)	Catholic (Total: 6)
Head Matron	Governor
Assist Matron	Storekeeper
Store Matron	2 Guardsmen
Hospital Matron	2 Servants
Reception Ward Matron	
Kitchen Matron	
Laundry Matron	
7 other Matrons	
Clerk	
Gatekeeper	
3 Guardsmen + messengers	
1 Servant	

Compiled from *Freeman's Journal*, 20 April 1847

Among the prisoners, however, Catholics far outnumbered other denominations (Table 3.8).

Table 3.8 Religious denomination of prisoners in Grangegorman and Richmond prisons, 1859.

	Catholic	Protestant	Presbyterian	% of Catholics
Grangegorman Penitentiary	1,964	28	3	89
Richmond Bridewell	1,173	131	12	89

Compiled from *Thirty-eighth report on the general state of prisons of Ireland,* H.C. 1860 xxxv, p. 51.

MARGARET AYLWARD AND THE ONSET OF SYNNOTT'S DIFFICULTIES

Synnott's work as governor was subjected to the usual scrutiny every year by visiting inspectors-general, and up to 1861 their reports generally attributed to him a high level of competence. Things , however, began to go wrong from that year, the time of Margaret Aylward's imprisonment there.[50]

Aylward was the foundress of St. Brigid's Orphanage in Dublin which in the 1860s was very much at the centre of Catholic resistance to the proselytising being carried out by Protestant associations. In November 1860 Aylward, suspected of preventing a woman from having access to her child, was committed for six months to Grangegorman prison. The child, Mary Matthews, had been received by the orphanage at the request of her dying father who feared the mother would have her reared in the Protestant faith.[51] Aylward was at first sent to the Richmond bridewell which the court seemed to forget was a male prison.[52] She was then transferred to Grangegorman where she spent the following six months. Synnott showed himself throughout the case to be a strong defender of Aylward while at the same time taking care to keep within the law. On 6 November 1860, in the court of Queen's Bench in Dublin, Synnott in line with the defence counsel, endeavoured to obtain special consideration for Aylward[53] thereby revealing, through the newspaper reports and through them to the inspectors-general, where his sympathies lay. While in Grangegorman, Aylward's health began to deteriorate. Her doctors declared her life in danger, and her legal representatives along with Synnott approached the chief justice at his house in March 1861. The justice informed Synnott: 'You will take care that anything which this lady requires shall be allowed her'. He also promised, if required, his written authority for any privileges granted.[54] Encouraged by this, the board voted that Aylward should have the privileges, which included the following: she could wear her own clothes, take exercise in the garden, have her own food, receive and send unopened mail, retain a key to her room, have visitors between 10 a.m. to 4 p.m. daily except Sundays, and her domestic servant was to be admitted to her twice each day.[55] When news of the privileges were leaked to the *Daily Express*, a Conservative Dublin newspaper,[56] Synnott came under more intense pressure, especially from the inspector-general of prisons, Corry Connellan, who, when he was made aware of the privileges, immediately appeared at the prison.[57] Corry Connellan, a Protestant Conservative, appeared zealous to uphold the letter of the law especially in the case of the privileges granted to Aylward. Prior to his appointment as inspector-general of prisons he had, like Marian Rawlins, worked in the lord lieutenant's household, as private secretary to the lord lieutenant.[58]

During Aylward's imprisonment, there appeared to be a 'Protestant' line of communication between the inspectorate and certain individuals in the city prisons, the board and the city council. It was through Rawlins that the details of the privileges granted to Aylward leaked from Grangegorman.[59] She informed her son, Arthur Rawlins, who in turn passed details on to John O. Bonsall, a Protestant Conservative on the city council.[60] The board of superintendence, being also responsible for the Richmond male prison where Arthur Rawlins was deputy governor, decided to dismiss him from his post for this breach of confidentiality.[61] Bonsall now, in a letter to Corry Connellan on 6 April 1861, asked to have Arthur Rawlins reinstated. Although not then on the board of superintendence, Bonsall felt that as a member of the municipal council which, along with the board and the lord lieutenant, shared responsibility for the city prisons, he was entitled to know the details of any rules adopted for the city prisons. The eight rules granted to Aylward were, according to him, designed to 'defeat the sentence of her Majesty's courts of law', and for purely 'sectarian' reasons. Bonsall also pointed out that it was not Rawlins but he who had decided to bring the matter to the public through the *Daily Express*.[62] Bonsall's letter reflects the religious feelings aroused by the Aylward case, and the complicated network of the sometimes politically conflicting authorities which managed the prison system in Dublin.

The Aylward case also brought into focus the question of who had the authority in the appointment and dismissal of prison officers. Connellan argued that it remained solely in the hands of the lord lieutenant while the board replied that it had exercised the power to dismiss for almost ten years.[63] The outcome was that Arthur Rawlins was reinstated but was soon after transferred to the governorship of Longford prison, 'of his own accord' as Connellan stressed,[64] but probably because of government pressure, in the hope of avoiding a confrontation over the issue.

In spite of the effects of prison life on her health, Margaret Aylward's strength of character did not diminish. This was no doubt partly due to the support she received from Synnott. She was unhappy with the deputy matron, Mary O'Carroll, who was unwilling to provide one of her rooms for Aylward's use, but noted in a letter addressed to O'Carroll that Synnott was quite ready to give her one of his, and reported him as saying 'Tho my family is large, I will give one most willingly'.[65] By contrast, O'Carroll's perceived unwillingness to do the same drew the stinging comment·

> May you enjoy every happiness in the room the passing use of which (tho declared necessary for my health) you have refused me, is the earnest & sincere wish dear Mrs. O'Carroll.[66]

Although Aylward did not send the above letter, it nevertheless indicates that the conflict here was not simply a sectarian one. O'Carroll was in fact a Catholic whose deceased husband had been a prominent Dublin Catholic and close acquaintance of Daniel Murray, the late Catholic archbishop of Dublin.[67] Many of the board who unanimously voted in favour of the privileges for Aylward, were Protestants.[68]

The inspector-general interrogated Synnott as to the circumstances concerning his visit to the chief justice, in particular as to whether he had leave from the board or any other official authority to make such a visit.[69] The written authority for the privileges was never in fact given, possibly because the public criticism aired by the *Daily Express* caused the chief justice to 'shuffle' (Aylward's word) out of his promise.[70] Connellan could have confirmed for himself without inconvenience the verbal authority of the chief justice, but chose instead to focus on the legality of Synnott's actions in the case. Synnott's sympathy was always with Aylward. In a letter to Paul Cullen, the Catholic archbishop of Dublin, on 25 March 1861 Aylward pointed to the possible pressure on Synnott. He was considered as

friendly to me – I should be sorry indeed that he would get any an-
noyance about it for he has been kind to me and has fortunately acted
according to rule in all.[71]

Corry Connellan did not agree. In his report for that year, he criticised Synnott
on a number of points. According to him, Synnott had violated that section
of the prison act which permitted a clergyman to replace a chaplain through
sickness or unavoidable absence. No fewer than four clergymen had been allowed into the prison to visit Aylward along with the chaplain. The visitors
which the Lord Chief Justice permitted Aylward to have could have included
clergy, but Connellan clearly did not accept this. In his official report for that
year he included the following criticism of Synnott.

> I cannot dismiss the consideration of this discreditable case without the
> strong expression of the opinion that throughout the Governor, Mr.
> Synnott, evinced a strong sense of partisanship.

A similar spirit in the future 'from whatever quarter' would bring the full
weight of the Prisons Act upon it, 'with a view to its suppression, and to the
removal of those who shall have thus transgressed.'[72]

The public criticism and ridicule to which Connellan was subjected in the
municipal council, where he was described as the 'court jester of the Vice-
Regal establishment' also got into the press,[73] and may also have hardened his
negative view of Synnott. Connellan also referred to other acts of indiscretion
on Synnott's part, for instance the employment of a former prisoner in his
household,[74] a bye-law infringement but considered by the board of superintendence at the time to have arisen from charitable motives.[75] The attempt by
Synnott to admit Timmons to visit his imprisoned wife, he considered to be
on 'perfectly futile grounds'.[76] Again the board sided with Synnott. Both these
complaints, which came after the Aylward case, reflect a distinct change in
Connellan's attitude to Synnott. The inspector-general completed his report
by making ominous reference to the 'anomaly'[77] of a male governor in a female prison originally intended to be run by females. Synnott had now incurred the displeasure of a very powerful government officer whose attitude
would be crucial if doubt arose in the lord lieutenant's mind as to his competence or integrity.

It was difficult to remain impartial in the Aylward case. What Connellan
saw as a 'strong spirit of partisanship' on Synnott's part was seen by Aylward as
gentlemanly kindness. The admission of four priests by Synnott into the
prison to visit Aylward was considered by Connellan as a serious breach of
prison rules but as 'too frivolous to comment on' by some members of the
city council.[78] While there is some evidence for the view that Marian Rawlins
was in league with Connellan against Synnott, most of the ill-feeling she had

towards Synnott arose from the threat his position as governor posed to her authority, rather than to religious bias. Rawlins did not sympathise with Aylward but neither did the deputy-matron of Grangegorman, Mary O'Carroll, a prominent Catholic. As is clear from the Timmons case, the female authority in the prison was also zealously guarded by O'Carroll.[79]

Criticism of Synnott came not only from the inspectors-general. The board of superintendence for 1863 discovered that Edward Dunne, the storekeeper in Grangegorman, had sold some prison rags and handed the prison book-keeper, Benjamen Warren, only part of the money received for the rags, retaining the remainder as a loan. Warren made only a pencil note of the transaction in his journal. The board learnt of this incident only at the end of their year in office and suspected that Synnott was deliberately keeping the information from them. Dunne was also in debt, and being in debt was likely to affect the proper discharge of his duties. Synnott should have made a note of this in his journal and reported it to the local inspector. The 1863 board also suspected that Synnott himself was in debt to some of his subordinate officers and was for that reason not strict enough with them. On the 30 December 1863, Synnott, along with Dunne and Warren, were suspended.[80] Boards were empowered to suspend any prison officer for misconduct, and could also dismiss an officer with the sanction of the lord lieutenant.[81] The next and final meeting of this board took place on the 30 December 1863, when the board recorded their approval of the suspensions and urged the succeeding board to continue the investigations into the accounts of Grangegorman which they had already begun. At this meeting Bonsall, who was a member of the board in 1863, along with another conservative Protestant named Vereker, made an attempt to amend the resolution to suspend Synnott with a proposal to have him dismissed.[82] They were the only members to support this amendment, the eight others, indicated in the table below, voting for the original resolution to suspend Synnott.

It would be wrong however to assume a clear denominational divide in the board regarding Synnott. One member, A.M. Sullivan a Catholic nationalist who was one of the auditors of the prison accounts that year, was also critical if not suspicious of Synnott's bookkeeping. He and another nationalist member, John Gray, proposed the suspension of Synnott and were supported by six others.[83] Those in favour of the suspension are highlighted in the table below. Bonsall and Vereker are not included in this list. The sources do not record them as having voted for the suspension, but presumably they did vote with the other eight once their amendment to dismiss Synnott had been defeated. Therefore the view as later implied by Synnott, that Connellan was the only source of his problems, is not accurate.[84]

The inspectors-general urged the incoming board for 1864 to appoint the city accountant, John Connolly, to investigate 'all the instances of default, suppression, misrepresentation and neglect; as well as the several relations of the officers one to another in pecuniary transactions'.[85] The incoming board

Table 3.9 Boards of superintendence for 1863 and 1864

For 1863	For 1864
J.P. Vereker, (Lord Mayor)	*Coun, P.P. McSwiney* (Lord mayor)
Ald. John Campbell, J.P.	*Alderman John Reynolds, J.P.*
Councillor Joseph Casson, J.P.	Ald. John Campbell, J.P.
Coun. Nicholas J. Lalor, J.P.	Coun. Nicholas J.Lalor, J.P.
Coun. Sir John Gray, J.P	*Coun. Robert O Brien, J.P.*
Coun. Jeremiah Dunne, J.P. (absent)	Coun.Jeremiah Dunne, J.P. (absent)
Ald. John O. Bonsall	*Coun. William Callan*
Ald. Richard Wilson	*Coun. Michael Egan*
Coun. Alexander M. Sullivan	*Coun. Joseph Sweetman*
Coun. Michael Murphy	*Coun. Richard Keating*
Coun. John Draper	Coun. John French
Coun. Edward Lawless (died in 1863)	Coun. John Ryan (absent)

Sources: Forty second report on a general state of prisons of Ireland, H.C. 1864 xxvii, pp 404–5. National Archives, Dublin, C.S.O.R.P. 23315 (1883). Those italicised in the list for 1863 voted to suspend Synnott. Those italicised in the list for 1864 voted to reinstate him. Bonsall and Vereker voted to dismiss Synnott, and probably voted also to suspend him although they are not recorded as having done the latter.

voted at its first meeting on the 20 January 1864, and after a 'full and minute investigation into all matters', to entirely acquit him of any intention to do or sanction any improper act, and to reinstate him immediately. Connellan doubted the ability of the board to carry out a thorough investigation in one day.[86] The board did however find that Synnott had been too lenient with his subordinate officers. He was warned to maintain due strictness with his staff, and to avoid 'mistaken leniency'. Dunne was also restored to his post, the board having found that his suspension was 'totally unwarranted by the facts'.[87] Warren was also cleared of criminal intent, but because of his advanced age was superannuated.

The 1864 board also complied with the request of the inspectors–general that the city accountant examine the accounts of the prison. Connellan accepted the accountant's findings but noted that his instructions were limited to seeking improvements in the manner of keeping the accounts. Although a number of printed copies of the accountant's report were made, I have been unable to locate any to date. However there are references to it in the report of the board to the municipal council. According to the board the accountant's investigation found that apart from the 'rags' incident all the imputations made against Synnott were groundless. The board were also unhappy with the manner in which Connellan called for an investigation by the city accountant in the first place, because it suggested the inspector-general had found Synnott guilty before the investigation had even begun.[88]

Only two members of the 1864 board voted against Synnott: Campbell[89] and Lalor. Apart from Jeremiah Dunne, Campbell and Lalor were the only two of this board who had been members of the 1863 board. Therefore through the luck of a lottery which decided the membership of this board, the pressure was lifted from Synnott. The fact that Corry Connellan noted negatively in his report the religious and political distribution of this board, suggests that he saw this as an important influence in Synnott's reinstatement.[90]

Connellan's report to parliament on Grangegorman prison for 1863 was extraordinarily long (nine pages of it dealt with the allegations against Synnott). To understand why, we must consider his prospective readership. The lord lieutenant would very likely have accepted the inspectors' advice. It would appear that Connellan's aim was to dent Synnott's long-standing good reputation by driving home to the board of 1864 and the city council that the support they gave to Synnott was not deserved. The length of the report may have been an unwitting acknowledgement by him of Synnott's popularity among Dublin politicians and other leading figures. In it Connellan detailed the charges against Synnott, and presented his own conclusions. Synnott had, according to Connellan, proved himself unfit to be governor after years of 'unavailing experience'. He had failed in the following areas: correct financial supervision, in not reporting all irregularities in the prison and in failing to enforce a strict discipline. Connellan questioned Synnott's integrity with the following words: 'and I regret to be constrained to add, that such is his normal inaccuracy of mind (to use no harsher a phrase) that it is impossible to place reliance on his statements, if unsupported'. Connellan considered the investigation by the city accountant to be inadequate because the board had limited the latter to merely suggesting ways of improving the bookkeeping system. He criticised the system of electing boards by lot because it meant that there was no continuity of experience, and this for example prevented the 1863 board from completing an investigation it had just started. Connellan felt that the 1864 board was inadequate not only because it contained an unusually large number of inexperienced members, but also because eleven of its members professed the 'same religious creed' and all shared the same 'political bias'. Connellan also stressed the importance of devising a method of selection which would ensure adequate representation on the board of the religious and political minority. Connellan referred also to the anomalous position of the governor in Grangegorman whose duties even if efficiently carried out would take only a fourth of the time of other gaols whose governors had the same salary.[91]

This account of Synnott's troubles in 1862–64 raises some questions. Was he the innocent casualty of a vengeful Connellan following the Aylward *debacle* in 1862? Were Connellan's actions coloured by religious and political prejudice? Was he merely motivated by a zeal to uphold the laws which applied to the prison system? To what extent was Synnott caught up in a power struggle between the nationalist city council and the government? Was

Synnott actually committing petty fraud which only came to light after a re-formed inspectorate fired by the Aylward case decided to maintain a closer sur-veillance on Synnott? In spite of the city accountant's exoneration of Synnott, Connellan continued to doubt his integrity. What happened in 1863 does not show conclusively that Synnott was engaged in petty fraud. Had they believed that he was committing fraud it is unlikely that the 1864 board would have exonerated Synnott simply because he was a Catholic and a nationalist. As we have seen, some of those on the 1863 board who doubted his integrity and who voted to actually suspend him, pending further investigation, were Catholic nationalists.

More charges were brought against Synnott in 1864. Some guns and pistols normally kept in the prison office were reported as missing by Charles P. Gavin, the local inspector of the Richmond and Grangegorman prisons. The guns were old and had been wrapped in a cloth with the pistols for some years. The police discovered that two of Synnott's sons had taken the guns in order to get some of them altered while using others as a means of paying for the alterations. No charges were brought against the sons. Presumably they were not suspected of anything other than using them for shooting pigeons in the prison yard, an explanation hinted at by their father who mentioned the damage done by pigeons to the paintwork in the prison. However in the Fenian-charged atmosphere of the time, the initial suspicions of the police were quite natural. The incident reflected more on Synnott's competence than his integrity. It provided more fuel for those hostile to him in the prison's inspectors office in Dublin Castle. Synnott was reprimanded and warned of the 'severest consequences if at any future time he shall be shown to be neg-ligent or remiss in the discharge of his duties'.[92] Another investigation that year concerned the suspicion that Synnott had ordered sherry wine from the prison store for his own use but contrived to ensure that the prison pay for it. The contradictory evidence[93] taken at the investigation into the incident was not conclusive of Synnott's guilt, but the series of complaints does suggests a close surveillance of Synnott since the Aylward case.

SYNNOTT'S DISMISSAL

The incident that finally led to Synnott's dismissal occurred in June 1865 and concerned a prisoner, Bridget Connolly, who had been sentenced to fourteen days without fine for assault but who was released by Synnott on the payment to him of a fine. Again the evidence was inconclusive as to whether Synnott had intended pocketing the money or was simply inefficient.[94] Synnott may have intended handing over the money. There is however an unexplained delay of nine days between Connolly's release from prison and the date the local inspector reported the matter to the board of superintendence. A serious matter like this would probably have been reported by the local inspector as soon as he became aware of it. If true, one wonders why Synnott delayed so long before reporting it. One would have expected that Synnott would have been more attentive to the regulations given the recent investigations and in particular the warnings following the missing guns in 1864. Perhaps the trust shown in him by the 1864 board had made him over-confident. The board members were lenient, recommending a severe reprimand, unlike the government who on 23 August 1865 directed the board to remove him from the governship of Grangegorman because of the repeated irregularities.[95] It must be said that the dismissal was based on perceived irregularities over the previous four years, which began by coincidence or otherwise with the Aylward case. It can be argued that the discovery of so many faults had to do with a more efficient prison inspectorate. However the efforts to effect a greater prison efficiency began before 1861, and the contrast between all the reports relating to Synnott prior to the Aylward case and those subsequent to it, is striking. The Aylward case, no doubt, aroused tensions between the inspectors-general and the Dublin municipal council. It did not necessarily follow that the council, or the board appointed by it, always sided with Synnott. But a majority in these bodies, during Synnott's time as governor, were sympathetic towards him. There appears sufficient reason to suppose that Synnott had become somewhat lax in his later years as governor. By the 1860s whatever novelty the position of governor originally had for him had worn off. There was also the ongoing frustration with the restraints imposed by his position as governor of a female prison. By 1865 Synnott was defiant after years of suspicion and investigations.

There were many on the municipal council and the board whose view of Synnott was in striking contrast to that of the inspectors-general. Was this due to his courteous personality and his longstanding popularity with Dublin politicians? Perhaps they doubted not his integrity but had come to recognise his increasing inefficiency. The board presented him with a glowing reference in August 1865 recognising his errors but believing that they were 'of the head not the heart', and they recommended that the council grant, and the lord lieutenant sanction, him superannuation for his eighteen years of service.[96] A second letter from the board included the statement that Synnott's moral character and integrity were above suspicion,[97] a judgement clearly contrary to Connellan's perception of him.

Synnott sought a tribunal to enquire into the circumstances of his dismissal, first from the lord lieutenant[98] and being refused by him Synnott then approached the municipal council.[99] The latter body agreed to recommend to the board to hold an enquiry, but on hearing the opinion of the law officers of the crown that the board would be acting illegally in holding such an enquiry and that they would be civilly and criminality responsible if they did so, they decided to proceed no further.[100]

The municipal council also trod a narrow path between a general sympathy for Synnott and a concern not to go beyond their jurisdiction. They would recommend that Synnott receive a retiring allowance but only 'if it can be legally done'.[101] The vote was overwhelming in favour and included two members of the 1863 board of superintendence (Sullivan and Gray) who at the time had voted for Synnott's suspension. Superannuation was however never granted. Some years later, Isaac Butt, the well-known Irish political figure and lawyer, made an unsuccessful attempt[102] in parliament to introduce an amendment to the prisons officer superannuation bill of 1873[103] which would have entitled Synnott to a pension.

Synnott's final attempt to be reinstated, but mainly to recover his good name, was through the courts, again without success.[104] The case centred on whether the lord lieutenant had the right to dismiss the governor of a city prison. Two interesting points emerge from the case. First, the crown and treasury solicitors acting on behalf of the government, the defendants, were not happy with the files presented for the case by the inspectors-general of prisons,[105] much to the embarrassed irritation of the inspectors-general.[106] The evidence presented to the solicitors appeared to them to be insufficient to prove misconduct on Synnott's part. Secondly, the basis of the court's eventual decision was not any misconduct of Synnott. The *Freeman's Journal* reported:

> His Lordship said that it was true that no imputation of misconduct was made against the plaintiff but there could be no doubt that the lord lieutenant under the statute possessed the power of dismissal at his will and pleasure, and without assigning any cause or instituting any enquiry.[107]

Therefore the absolute power of the government in the dismissal of prison officers was the issue in this court, not any irregularities of Synnott. The judge may have been influenced by the prevailing Fenian atmosphere and in particular the escape of the Fenian leader, James Stephens, in 1865.[108]

> The escape of one prisoner might lead to the escape of many, especially in a time of great political commotion and if the Lord Lieutenant could not act without an enquiry it might happen that before that enquiry terminated all the prisoners had been set at large.[109]

Synnott's career and good name were, it appears from this summing-up, secondary to the maintenance of law and order.

Synnott's name disappeared from the government and city council records after 1870. His precarious financial situation can be tentatively linked to a letter sent to him from Clonmel in 1876 which refers to a planned meeting at which subscriptions would be made and at which Synnott's presence would be crucial for its successful outcome. All the local clergy, the writer claimed, would subscribe. Unfortunately nothing has been found to enlighten us further here.[110] It is an interesting point, given his former role in famine relief, that no reference apart from this has been found of any effort being made by the Catholic clergy to support or plead for Synnott. Legal problems between Synnott and a trustee to the will of his second wife, who left her fairly substantial wealth to the only surviving child of this marriage, suggest encroachment by Synnott on the estate in order to meet expenses incurred in his court case.[111]

The double-fronted two-storey house in fashionable Sandymount in Dublin, where Synnott lived from 1872 until his death in 1897, displays middle-class respectability rather than pecuniary embarrassment.[112] While resident there Synnott was president of a parish committee welcoming home their parish priest, John O'Hanlon, from Rome.[113] Perhaps his reputation had been restored somewhat in his last years. An obituary on Synnott might have provided a contemporary view of his career, but none has been found. The absence of any such comment indicates that the public memory of Synnott's achievements had not survived into his old age.

Conclusion

It is difficult to know the truth of the inspectors-general suspicions about Synnott's integrity. It is also difficult to avoid the conclusion that Synnott was not really suited to the position of prison governor. His undoubted qualities as bookkeeper and communicator, exemplified in his work in the great famine, were important. On the other hand the frequent reference to his kindness and courtesy perhaps belie in his case a lack of firmness necessary for the management of a nineteenth-century prison. The position of prison governor of a large city prison gave him a certain status, but it was not quite matched by a salary commensurate with his standard of living. The unsatisfactory management structure within the prison meant relatively few responsibilities for him and a consequent smaller salary. It also made him vulnerable to attack from other senior officers intent on preserving and even increasing their power base. In the turmoil surrounding the Aylward case, Synnott's increasing tendency to be inattentive to prison rules and his perceived links with local nationalist politicians, ultimately contributed to his downfall as governor of Grangegorman.

It does appear that Synnott never quite realised his potential as was indicated in his work in famine relief. Grangegorman prison with its 'anomaly' had little to offer and its long term prospects for the governor were not good. In 1869 rationalisation by the authorities led to a reduction of staff in that prison to twenty-two[1] from thirty-five in 1863.[2] Perhaps if he had taken the route of his political allies of the 1840s (e.g. Arkins, Bury and Gardiner) and followed a career in city politics or/and in commerce, he might have fared better. However, although assisted no doubt by a comfortable background, Synnott did manage to achieve much in local Dublin politics, and his involvement in famine relief appears to have been the high point of an interesting and somewhat tragic life.

This study shows how complex could be the life of a middle-class Catholic in nineteenth-century Ireland. The personal and political loyalties and antipathies were not always drawn simply along religious and ideological lines. Other emotions and needs often made up what was a complex fabric of life. This study does not represent the full story, nor exactly as Synnott and his contemporaries might have told it. However it is hoped that it has achieved its objective of producing a coherent picture of Synnott in the communities in which he lived.

Notes

A.H.	*Archivium Hibernicum*
D.C.A.	Dublin City Archives
D.D.A.	Dublin Diocesan Archives
D.E.M.	*Dublin Evening Mail*
D.E.P.	*Dublin Evening Post*
E.F.	*Evening Freeman*
E.P.	*Evening Post*
F.J.	*Freeman's Journal*
H.F.A.	Holy Faith Archives, Dublin
I.H.S.	*Irish Historical Studies*
M.R.	*Morning Register*
N.A.	National Archive of Ireland
N.L.I.	National Library of Ireland
R.C.B.	Representative Church Body Library

INTRODUCTION

All maps used are reproduced from the Map Library, Trinity College Library Dublin, with the permission of the Board of Trinity College.

1 The famine papers are in the Dublin Diocesan Archives under 'Murray papers', and have been calendered in *A.H.*, xxxix (1984), pp 62–87; xl (1985), pp 35–114; xli (1986), pp 3–63 and xlii (1987), pp 49–105.

2 Mary Purcell, 'Highlights on Dublin diocesan archives', *A.H.*, xxxvi (1981), p. 47.

3 As distinct from the hundreds of local parish voluntary relief committees set up during this famine which are not under consideration in this study.

4 Margaret Gibbons, *Life of Margaret Aylward* (London, 1928) pp 167–87.

5 J. O' Rourke, *The history of the great famine of 1847 with notices of earlier Irish famines* (3rd. ed., Dublin, 1902), p. 67.

6 Desmond Bowen, *Souperism: myth or reality? A study of Catholics and Protestants during the great famine* (Dublin, 1970), e.g. pp 118–9.

7 Donal Kerr, *A nation of beggars?: priest, people and politics in famine Ireland 1846–1852* (Oxford, 1994), p. 38.

8 David Sheehy, 'Archbishop Murray of Dublin and the great famine in Mayo', *Cathair na Mart, journal of the Westport historical society*, xi (1991, Mayo), pp 118–28.

9 J.R. Hill, 'Nationalism and the Catholic church in the 1840s: views of Dublin repealers', *I.H.S.*, xix (1975), p. 371–95. Mary E. Daly, *Dublin: the deposed capital, 1860–1914* (Cork, 1985), esp. chapter seven.

10 N.A., C.S.O.R.P., (1883), 23315.

11 Rena Lohan, 'The treatment of women sentenced to transportation and penal servitude, 1790–1898' unpublished M.Litt. thesis, Trinity College, Dublin, 1993.

12 O'Donnell to Murray, 13 April 1848 (D.D.A., Murray papers, 55/32/4).

13 R.D. Edwards and T.D. Williams, (eds.) *The great famine: studies in Irish history, 1845–1852* (Dublin, 1956).

14 C. Woodham Smith, *The great hunger: Ireland 1845–49* (London, 1962).

15 Mary E. Daly, *The famine in Ireland* (Dundalk, 1986).

16 Christine Kinealy, *This great calamity, the Irish famine 1845–52* (Dublin, 1994).

17 J.S. Donnelly, 'The administration of relief, 1846–7', 'The administration of relief, 1847–51', both in W.E. Vaughan (ed.), *A New History of Ireland, v: 'Ireland under the union, 1, 1801–70'* (Oxford, 1989).

SYNNOTT AND ST. PAUL'S THE EARLY YEARS: 1830–48

1 Registry of burials, Prospect Cemetery, grave T.A. 25 251/2.

2 It was only from 1834 that Dublin directories included streets with names of residents, and this has limited our knowledge of the Synnotts before the 1830s.

3 Records of St. Paul's parish, now kept in the nearby Halston street parish.

4 *An alphabetical list of the constituency of the city of Dublin with the residence qualification and profession of each voter, and the votes given at the elections of 1832, 1835, 1837.* Printed by a committee of messrs. Hamilton and West (Dublin, n.d.)

5 Mary E. Daly, *Dublin the deposed capital, 1860–1914* (Cork, 1985), p. 204. Synnott's father is not included in a printed list of freemen of the city of Dublin, *An alphabetical list of the freemen of the city of Dublin, 1774–1823* (n.p.,n.d.).

6 *F.J.*, 27 Jan 1847.

7 The family business addresses can be traced through *Pettigrew and Oulton, Dublin almanac and general register of Ireland, 1834–43*, and in *Thom's Irish almanac and official directory* from 1844. [hereafter cited as *Thom's directory*]

8 Louis M. Cullen: 'The growth of Dublin 1600–1900: character and heritage' in F.H.A. Aalen and Kevin Whelan (ed.), *Dublin city and county: from prehistory to present* (Dublin, 1992), pp 252–3.

9 *E.P.*, 25 Oct 1845.

10 Compiled from *Second report of the commissioners appointed to investigate the state of education*, app (parochial abstracts) H.C., 1826–7(12), xii.1, pp 558–61.

11 *First report of Select committee on state of disease, and condition of labouring poor, in Ireland*, (314) H.C., 1819, viii, 365 p. 78.

12 Application for loans, Cholera papers 1832–34, N.A., 2/440/8.

13 Registry of deeds, Dublin, 1835/19/23.

14 *F.J.*, 19 Dec 1846.

15 Registry of deeds, Dublin, 1835/19/23.

16 For more on Mathew see Moira Lysaght,. *Fr. Theobald Mathew, OFM Cap., the apostle of temperance* (Dublin, 1983).

17 Prospect cemetery, Dublin, Grave T.A. 25 251/2.

18 Synnott grave.

19 Henry Shaw, *The Dublin pictorial guide and directory of 1850* (2nd ed., Dublin, 1988).

20 e.g. *F.J.*, 16 Nov 1839.

21 *F.J.*, 11 June 1839.

22 *Memorial of grocers in Ireland respecting clause relating to sale of spirits by grocers*, (479) H.C., 1836, xlv. 653.

23 *Bill to suspend so much of act of 1836 as prohibits holding of licenses for sale of spirits by retail, by grocers in Ireland,* (606) H.C., 1837–38, vi. 391.

24 *F.J.,* 17 June 1839.

25 *F.J.,* 17 June 1839.

26 *Thom's directory,* 1839, p. 330.

27 *E.F.,* 19 March 1840.

28 Compiled from *Thom's directories.*

29 *F.J.,* 11 June 1839. O'Connell's support for the vintners and grocers is evident in a letter from O'Connell to P.V. Fitzpatrick in Maurice O'Connell (ed.), *The correspondence of Daniel O'Connell* (8 vols., Dublin. n.d.), v, p. 381.

30 *Bill for relief of H. M. Roman Catholic subjects,* H.C. 1829 (73) 11. 1.

31 Donald Akenson, *The Church of Ireland: ecclesiastical reform and revolution, 1800–1885* (New Haven and London, 1971), pp 52–4.

32 Donald H. Akenson, *The Church of Ireland* pp 52–4.

33 St. Paul's Church of Ireland, vestry minutes, e.g., 1838: officer of health, (p. 72); 1841: apploter, (p. 102); 1836: parish constable (p. 138), R.C.B., P 273/6/6.

34 See for example criticism by Thomas Arkins of appointment of wardens, *F.J.* 25 March 1848, and dispute in St Mark's parish which led to acceptance there that appointments of wardens lay solely in Protestant hands, *F.J.,* 5 March 1840. See also Jacqueline Hill, *From patriots to unionists: Dublin civic politics and Irish Protestant patriotism, 1660–1849* (forthcoming).

35 St. Paul's Church of Ireland, vestry minutes, p 22, R.C.B., P 273/6/6.

36 *F.J.,* 2 April 1839.

37 *M.R.,* 29 March 1842.

38 *F.J.,* 6 April 1839.

39 *F.J.,* 18 May 1839.

40 *F.J.,* 18 May 1839.

41 *F.J.,* 21 May 1839

42 *F.J.,* 8 Nov 1841.

43 *F.J.,* 18 April 1843.

44 Jacqueline Hill, 'Nationalism and the catholic church in the 1840s: views of Dublin repealers' in *I.H.S.,* xix, (1975–6), p. 373.

45 *M.R.,* 9 Aug 1842.

46 Daniel O'Connell, *Instructions to wardens* (May, 1843).

47 *Bill for more effective relief of destitute poor in Ireland* [as amended in committee, and on recommitment], H.C., 1837–38 (238), v. 345.

48 *F.J.,* 5 July 1839.

49 Virginia Crossman, *Local government in nineteenth century Ireland* (Belfast, 1994), p. 47.

50 *F.J.,* 15 July 1839. *D.E.M.,* 12 July 1839.

51 *F.J.,* 19 July 1839.

52 *F.J.,* 19 July 1839.

53 *F.J.,* 22 June 1839.

54 *F.J.,* 15 July 1839.

55 *M.R.,* 18 Aug 1842.

56 *D.E.P.,* 12 May 1840.

57 Compiled from minute books of north Dublin union, (Dr. Steeven's hospital, Dublin).

58 Alexander Thom, *Dublin Directory* (1842), p. 286.

59 *M.R.,* 23 April 1842.

60 *Thom's Directory,* 1848, p. 924; 1849, p. 1034.

61 Edward Keane, P. Beryl Phair and Thomas U. Sadleir (eds) *King's Inns admission papers 1607–1867* (Dublin, 1982).

62 George D. Burchaell and Thomas U. Sadleir (eds.) *Dublin University alumni, a register of the students, graduates, professors and provosts of Trinity college, in the University of Dublin* (London, 1924).

63 e.g., North Dublin union minute book, 24 August 1839, (Dr. Steeven's hospital, Dublin).

64 *M.R.,* 20 Feb 1840.

65 *F.J.,* 2 Feb 1843. See also correspondence on the case in N.A., C.S.O.R.P., 016634 (1842).

66 *F.J.,* 25 March 1841.

67 *E.F.*, 1 Aug 1840.

68 *F.J.*, 2 March 1842. Minutes of municipal council, Nov 1841–Nov 1842. D.C.A., C2/A1/11, p. 81a.

69 *A digest of the act of the regulation of municipal corporations in Ireland*, by a barrister (Dublin, 1841).

70 *D.E.P.*, 2 April 1842. See also *Correspondence between lord. lieutenant of Ireland, Ulster king of arms, home secretary and garter king of arms on precedence between corporations of Dublin and Edinburgh in presenting addresses to queen or royal family*, H.C., 1863 (495) l. 679.

71 *M.R.*, 3 March 1842.

72 *F.J.*, 2 March 1842.

73 *M.R.*, 3 March 1842.

74 *D.E.M.*, 2 March 1842.

75 *F.J.*, 2 March 1842.

76 Minutes of municipal council, 22 Aug. 1848, D.C.A., C2/A1/14, p. 299.

77 *F.J.*, 2 March 1842. The debate on Synnott's selection is reported at length in this edition, and in *M.R.*, 3 March 1842.

78 Charles Chenvix Trench, *The great Dan, a biography of Daniel O'Connell* (London, 1983), p.187.

79 Minutes of municipal council, D.C.A., 1 March 1842, C2/A1/11, p.81a.

80 D.C.A., 21 Nov 1843. C2/A1/12 p. 368.

81 D.C.A., 22 Aug 1848. C2/A1/14 p.299.

82 D.C.A., C2/A1/13, p. 68, p.137, p.194, p.218, p.306, p.411, p.441.

83 Collections of documents concerning the suppression of O'Connell's monster repeal meeting at Clontarf, 1843 (Murray papers, D.D.A., 30/32/1).

SYNNOTT AND VOLUNTARY
FAMINE RELIEF, 1845–50

1 Synnott's position as secretary to these committees is referred to in Testimonials of character of Thomas L. Synnott, N.A., C.S.O.R.P., 1883, 23315 (hereafter cited as 'Testimonials of Synnott').

2 *Indian relief report*, p. 6; *Report of the proceedings of the general central relief committee for all Ireland on the 29 December 1846 to 31 December 1847* (Dublin, 1848), p. 8.

3 cf. reference in favour of Synnott from the chairman and honorary secretaries of the general central relief committee for all Ireland, 6 Sept. 1849, in 'Testimonials of Synnott'.

4 *Report of the Trustees of the Indian Relief Fund* (Dublin,1847), [hereafter cited as *Indian Relief report*]; Donal A.Kerr,'*A nation of beggars'? priests, people and politics in famine Ireland 1846–1852* (Oxford, 1994), p 46; W. P. O'Brien, *The great famine in Ireland and a retrospect of fifty years 1845–92* (London, 1896), pp 156–206; John O'Rourke, *The history of the great Irish famine* (3rd ed. Dublin, 1902), pp 508–513; *The report of the ladies' relief association for Ireland 1846–1850* (Dublin, 1850); *Irish relief association for the destitute peasantry* (Dublin, 1847).

5 The famine letters relating to the distribution of Catholic relief by Murray are in the Dublin Diocesan archive under 'Murray papers', and have been calendered in *A.H.* xxxix (1984), pp 62–87, xl (1985), pp 35–114, xli (1986), pp3–63 and xlii (1987), pp 49–105.

6 Trustees of the Indian relief fund to Synnott, (n.d.) in 'Testimonials of Synnott'.

7 *D.E.P.*, 2 December 1845.

8 Kevin B. Nowlan, 'The political background' in R. Dudley Edwards and T. Desmond Williams (eds.), *The great famine, studies in Irish history, 1845–52* (2nd. ed., Dublin,1994), p. 136.

9 *D.E.P.*, 2 Dec 1845.

10 *F.J.*, 13 Feb 1846.

11 *E.P.*, 1 Jan 1846.

12 *F.J.*, 13 Feb 1846. *D.E.P.*, 19 Feb 1846.

13 *F.J.*, 18 Dec 1845.

14 *D.E.M.*, 4 April 1846.

15 *D.E.P.*, 19 Feb 1846.

16 O 'Connell to Heytesbury, 27 July 1846 in 'Testimonials of Synnott'.

17 *D.E.M.*, 7 April 1846.

18 *Indian relief report*, pp 2–4.

19 See for example *Irish relief association for the destitute peasantry* (Dublin, 1847), p. 16.

20 *D.E.P.*, 16 April 1846.

21 *F.J.*, 3 June 1846.

22 Calculated from Synnott's analysis in *Indian relief report*.

23 *Indian relief report*, p. 21.

24 *Indian relief report*, p. 5.

25 *Central relief committee report* for July 1848–September 1849, p. 7–8.

26 *D.E.P.*, 17 Sept 1846.

27 *Indian relief report*, pp 5–6.

28 Mary E. Daly, *The famine in Ireland* (Dundalk, 1986), p. 90.

29 *Indian relief report*, p. 23.

30 *D.E.P.*, 31 July 1847.

31 Trustees of the Indian relief fund to Synnott, n.d., in 'Testimonials of Synnott'.

32 *D.E.P.*, 23 Dec 1846.

33 Reference in favour of Synnott from chairman and honorary secretaries of general central relief committee for all Ireland, 6 Sept 1849 in 'Testimonials of Synnott'.

34 *Report of the Proceedings of the General Famine Relief Committee of the Royal Exchange, from 3 May to 3 September 1849,* (Dublin,1849), p.37 (hereafter cited as *Royal Exchange committee report*).

35 Murray to Synnott, 7 November 1849 in 'Testimonials of Synnott'.

36 *Central relief committee report* for 1 July 1848 to 1 September 1849, p. 8.

37 W.J. Fitzpatrick, *The life, times and contemporaries of Lord Cloncurry* (Dublin, 1855), pp 507–8.

38 *D.E.P.*, 5 and 7 June 1849.

39 Peter O'Dwyer, 'John Francis Spratt, O. Carm., 1796–1871' unpublished PhD. thesis, Pontificia Universita Gregoriana, Rome, 1968, scrapbook A, p. 120.

40 Kerr, *A nation of beggars*, p. 59.

41 *Central relief committee report* for 29 December 1846 to 31 December 1847, p. 11.

42 ibid.

43 Synnott to lord mayor, 20 August 1847 (Hamilton papers, D.D.A., 151/37/1).

44 *Central relief committee report* for 1 July 1848 to 1 September 1848, n.p.

45 Christine Kinealy, *This great calamity, the Irish famine 1845–52* (Dublin, 1994), p. 336.

46 *Central Relief committee report* for 29 December 1846 to 31 December 1847, p. 19.

47 Mark Tierney, 'A short-title calendar of the papers of Archbishop Michael Slattery' in *Collectanea Hibernica*, nos. 34 and 35 (1992/3), p. 146.

48 *Royal exchange committee report*, p. 51.

49 *Central relief committee report*, 29 Dec. 1846 to 30 Dec. 1847, p. 8.

50 *Central relief committee report*,1 July 1848 to 1 Sept 1849, p. 9.

51 *D.E.P.*, 3 July 1847.

52 *Central relief committee report*, 29 December 1846 to 30 December 1847, p. 4.

53 Murray to Synnott, 7 November 1949 in 'Testimonials of Synnott'.

54 Tierney, 'Papers of Michael Slattery', p. 146.

55 The Murray famine correspondence have been calendered in *A.H.* xxxix (1984), pp 62–87, xl (1985), pp 35–114, xli (1986), pp 3–63; xlii (1987), pp 49–105.

56 See W. Meagher, *Notes on the life and character of his Grace, Most Reverend Daniel Murray, late archbishop of Dublin ... with historical and biographical notes* (Dublin, 1853).

57 Flannelly to Synnott, 27 June 1848 (Murray papers, D.D.A., 114/32/4).

58 Kerr, *A nation of beggars?* p. 59. An earlier estimate of £150,000 was made by Mary Purcell, 'Highlights on Dublin diocesan archives': *A.H.*, xxxvi (1981), p. 47.

59 1847 Murray Papers, D.D.A., 34/12

60 *Report of general central relief committee for all Ireland*, 29 December 1846 to 24 September 1849, (Dublin, 1849).

61 O'Carroll to Murray, 20 July 1847 (Murray Papers, D.D.A., 139/32/3).

62 Tierney, 'Papers of Michael Slattery', p. 146.

63 1847 Murray papers, D.D.A., 34/12.

64 This conflict is discussed in Kerr, *A nation of beggars*, pp 64–68.

65 Ward to Synnott, 5 March 1849 (Murray Papers, D.D.A., 132/32/5).

66 Byrne to Synnott, 13 March 1849 (Murray papers, D.D.A., 144/32/5).

67 Mary E. Daly, *The famine in Ireland* (Dundalk, 1986), p. 114.

68 Synnott to Murray, 15 July 1848 (Murray Papers, D.D.A., 120/32/4).

69 Mary Purcell, 'Highlights on Dublin Diocesan Archives', *A.H.*, xxxvi (1981), p. 47.

70 Browne to Murray, 6 July 1848 (Murray Papers, D.D.A., 118/32/4).

71 Browne to Murray, 13 March 1849 (Murray papers, D.D.A., 139/32/5).

72 Reference in Synnott's favour from the honorary secretaries of the central relief committee, 6 September 1849, Testimonials of Synnott, N.A., C.S.O.R.P., 1883, 23315.

SYNNOTT AND GRANGEGORMAN FEMALE PRISON, 1848–65

1 For an insight into the convict prisoners of Grangegorman see Rena Lohan, 'The treatment of women sentenced to transportation and penal servitude 1790–1898' unpublished M.Litt. thesis, Trinity College, Dublin, 1993.

2 Redington to Synnott, 12 May 1848 in Testimonials of Synnott, N.A., C.S.O.R.P., 1883, 23315.

3 Duke of Leinster to Corry Connellan, 26 Nov 1847 in 'Testimonials of Synnott.'

4 G.N. Wright, *An historical guide to ancient and modern Dublin* (2nd ed., London, 1825), pp 118–9.

5 *Twenty-eighth report on general state of prisons of Ireland*, 1850 H.C., [1229] xxix 305, p. 28 (hereafter cited as *Twenty-eighth rep.*).

6 Francis Johnston's original drawings of Richmond penitentiary (Irish Architectural Archive, Murray collection, 424–433).

7 *Bill for converting Richmond penitentiary into prison for Dublin, and amending laws relating to prisons in Ireland*, H.C., 1836 (421), iv. 733.

8 Registers of Prospect cemetery; Baptism registers of St. Paul's R.C. church.

9 Board of superintendence minutebook, 1864–65, D.C.A., BSP/1/8, pp 156 and 182.

10 *Forty-second report on general state of prisons of Ireland*, H.C., 1864 [3377] xxviii, p. 412 (hereafter cited as *forty-second report*).

11 *ibid.*, p. 411.

12 *D.E.P.*, 13 Dec 1845.

13 *Forty-second report*, p. 411–2.

14 *Twenty-seventh report on general state of prisons of Ireland*, H.C., 1849, [1069] xxvi. 373, p. 34 (hereafter cited as *Twenty-seventh report*).

15 *Papers relating to appointment of board of commissioners for management of government convict prisons in Ireland; and dismissal or removal from office of officers entrusted with management previous to passing of act*, H.C., 1854–55 (29) xlvii. 559, pp 1–4.

16 Register of Prospect cemetery, Dublin, 15 Nov 1886.

17 Minutes of Municipal Council, 2
Dec. 1857–5 Sept 1859, D.C.A.,
CA/A1/20, p.359.

18 *Forty-second report*, p. 396.

19 Synnott to board, 26 Nov. 1861 in
D.C.A. letter-book, Richmond
Female Penitentiary (n.p.).

20 *Twenty-eighth report*, pp 27 and 31.

21 *Sixteenth report on general state of prisons of Ireland*, H.C., 1837–38 (186)
xxxix. 475, p. 20.

22 e.g. *Twenty-ninth report on general state of prisons of Ireland*, H.C., 1851
[1364] xxviii. 357, p. 13.

23 Margaret Gibbons, *The life of Margaret Aylward* (Dublin,1928), p. 171.

24 *Forty-third report on general state of prisons of Ireland*, H.C., 1865 [3522]
xxiv.i, pp 462–3 (hereafter cited as *forty-third report*).

25 See note 7 above.

26 *Sixteenth report*, p. 22.

27 *Twenty-seventh report*, p. 37.

28 *Twenty-eighth report*, p. 27.

29 *ibid.*, pp 31–2.

30 *Twenty-ninth report*, p. 12.

31 Synnott to Gavin 9 Feb 1862 in
D.C.A. Letter-book, Richmond
Female Penitentiary, (n.p.). Board of
superintendence minute-book,
1862–3, D.C.A., BSP/1/7, pp 2–3.

32 See below 'Margaret Aylward and
the onset of Synnott's difficulties',
p. 57.

33 Register of applications for appointment in government prisons,
1847–56, N.A. G.P.B., bundle no. 25.

34 Hitchens to Synnott, 24 Nov. 1851
in 'Testimonials of Synnott'.

35 For a description (albeit subjective)
of the duties of the inspectors-general see *Report of the inspectors-general of prisons in Ireland to lord lieutenant, with regard to escape of James Stephens*, H.C., 1866 (147), lviii, 479, pp 32–3.

36 e.g. Synnott to Hitchens, 4 Dec.
1855, N.A., G.P.O. correspondence,
Grangegorman, 1855, carton 13, no.
965.

37 *Thirtieth report on general state of prisons of Ireland*, H.C., 1852 [1531]
xxvi, p. 61.

38 Minutes of municipal council, Aug.
1862–Sept. 1863, D.C.A.,
CA/A1/23, pp 39–42.

39 Synnott to Government Prisons
Office, 11 June 1855, N.A., G.P.O.
correspondence, Grangegorman,
1855, carton 10, no.43.

40 Register of burials, Prospect cemetery T.A. 25 251/2.

41 Armstrong to Synnott, 31 Aug.
1851, N.A., G.P.O. correspondence,
Grangegorman, 1851, carton 1, no.
807.

42 Board of superintendence minute
book, 1860–61–62, D.C.A., pp. 116–
121.

43 Synnott and Rawlins (in joint
memorial) to lord lieutenant, 10
Nov. 1853, N.A., G.P.O. correspondence, Grangegorman, 1853, carton
4, no. 61.

44 Hitchens to lord lieutenant, ibid.
According to himself, Synnott
earned £400 p.a. before his appointment as governor, Synnott to
board, 26 Nov 1861 in D.C.A.
Letter-book, Richmond female
penitentiary (n.p.).

45 Compiled from returns to Directors
of Prisons, N.A., G.P.O. Carton 14,
1856. Dublin prisons board report
(Dublin, 1869), p. 59.

46 Gavin to board, 21 Jan 1864 in board
of superintendence minute book,
1864–5, D.C.A., BSP/1/8, p. 330.

47 Petition book, no. 4, 11 Aug
1865–28 Dec 1868, N.A., T.1348.

48 Manuscript of government case
against Synnott, N.A., C.S.O.R.P.
1883, 23315.

49 *Forty-second report*, pp 402–3.

50 For more on Aylward see Margaret
Gibbons, *Life of Margaret Aylward*,
(Dublin,1900); Jacinta Prunty,
'Margaret Louisa Aylward
(1810–99)' in Mary Cullen and

Maria Luddy (eds), *Women, power and consciousness in 19th century Ireland* (Dublin, 1995), pp 71–3.

51 J. Prunty, 'Margaret Louisa Aylward', pp 71–3.

52 *F.J.*, 9 Nov. 1860.

53 ibid. Synnott's involvement in the Aylward case is referred to many times in Governor's Journal, Grangegorman female prison, D.C.A., January 1859–February 1964, pp 164–99.

54 Synnott to Nagle, 21 March 1861 in Letterbook, Richmond female penitentiary, D.C.A., n.p. Board of superintendence minute book, 1860–61–62, D.C.A., BSP/1/6, p. 220.

55 Board of superintendence minute book, 1860–61–62, D.C.A., BSP/1/6, p. 178.

56 *Daily Express*, 20 March 1861. This 1,600 word criticism of Aylward's privileges attacked the board but made no reference to Synnott.

57 Gibbons, *Life of Margaret Aylward*, pp 176–7.

58 Gibbons, *Life of Margaret Aylward*, p. 171.

59 Aylward to Cullen, 6 April 1861 (Cullen papers, D.D.A., 14/333/8).

60 Bonsall to Connellan, 6 April 1861, N.A., C.S.O.R.P. 1864, 19285.

61 Board of Superintendence minute book, 1860–61–62, D.C.A., BSP/1/6, p. 237.

62 Bonsall to Connellan, 6 April 1861, N.A., C.S.O.R.P. 1864, 19285.

63 *Fortieth report on general state of prisons of Ireland*, 1862 [3020] xxvi.i, p. 380 (hereafter cited as *Fortieth report*). Rough minutes of board of superintendence meeting, 15 Feb. 1851, N.A., C.S.O.R.P. 1864, 19285.

64 *Fortieth report*, p. 380.

65 Aylward to O'Carroll, 7 March 1861 (not sent), H.F.A., 1861/27/ma.ch/02.

66 ibid.

67 O'Carroll was the widow of Redmond Peter O'Carroll, first president of the society of St. Vincent de Paul in Ireland. O Carroll to Murray, 24 June 1847, (Murray papers, D.D.A., 26/32/3).

68 Gibbons, *Life of Margaret Aylward*, p. 171.

69 Governor's journal, January 1859–February 1864, D.C.A., p. 199.

70 Aylward to Cullen, 25 March 1861, (Cullen papers, D.D.A., 14/333/8).

71 ibid.

72 *Fortieth report*, pp 388–9.

73 Untitled cut-out from a contemporary newspaper, N.A., C.S.O.R.P. 1883, 23315.

74 *Fortieth report*, p. 389.

75 Board of superintendence minute book, 1860–61–62, D.C.A., p. 314.

76 *Fortieth report*, p. 389.

77 *Fortieth report*, p. 389.

78 Untitled cut-out of contemporary newspaper, N.A., C.S.O.R.P. 1883, 23315.

79 Extract from O'Carroll's prison journal, 14 Feb. 1862, N.A., C.S.O.R.P. 1883, 23315.

80 *Forty-second report*, pp 404–5. Board of superintendence minute-book, 1862–3, D.C.A., BSP/1/7, p. 304.

81 *Rules and regulations for the city of Dublin prisons prepared in conformity with the passing of the acts now in force* (Dublin, 1862), p. 3.

82 Rough minutes of board of superintendence meeting, N.A., C.S.O.R.P. 1883, 23315.

83 Board of superintendence minute book, 1862–63, D.C.A., BSP/1/7, p. 314.

84 '...my character which has been traduced by that functionary Mr.Corry Connellan...' from Synnott's schedule as an insolvent debtor referred to in government notes on his dismissal. N.A., C.S.O.R.P. 1883, 23315.

85 *Forty-second report*, p. 405.

86 ibid. Rough minutes of board of superintendence meeting, (n.d.), N.A., C.S.O.R.P. 1883, 23315.

87 *Forty-second report*, pp 405–6.
88 Report of the board of superinten-
    dence to the lord mayor, aldermen
    and burgesses of borough of Dublin,
    Board of superintendence minute
    book, Oct 1863–May 1864, D.C.A.,
    pp 343–5.
89 John Campbell. His vote was crucial
    in the controversial promotion of
    Arthur Rawlins to the newly-cre-
    ated position of deputy-governor of
    the Richmond bridewell, Aylward
    to Cullen, 25 March 1861 (Cullen
    papers, D.D.A., 14/333/8).
90 *Forty-second report*, p. 412.
91 *Forty-second report*, pp 397–412.
92 Dublin police report; Lentaigne's in-
    vestigation, N.A., C.S.O.R.P. 1883,
    23315.
93 Notes of investigation by Lentaigne
    at Grangegorman, 10 Aug. 1864.
    N.A. C.S.O.R.P. 1883, 23315. Board
    of superintendence minute book,
    1862–63, D.C.A., BSP/1/7,
    pp 381–2.
94 *Forty-fourth report on general state of
    prisons of Ireland*, H.C., 1866 [3690]
    xxxiv. 235, pp 484–5. Synnott to
    board, 28 June 1865 in 'Proceedings
    with reference to the dismissal of
    Thomas L. Synnott as governor of
    Grangegorman', N.A., C.S.O.R.P.
    1883, 23315.
95 *Forty-fourth report*, p. 485.
96 Copy of resolution of board of su-
    perintendence passed on the receipt
    of the letter directing removal of
    Thomas L. Synnott from governor-
    ship dated 23 Aug 1865, N.A.,
    C.S.O.R.P. 1883, 23315.
97 Testimonial by John Ryan, chair-
    man of the board of superinten-
    dence, 11 Oct. 1865, N.A.,
    C.S.O.R.P. 1883, 23315.
98 The humble and most respectful
    memorial of Thomas L. Synnott,
    late governor of Grangegorman

prison, N.A., C.S.O.R.P. 1883,
    23315.
99 Board of superintendence minute
    book, 1866–7, D.C.A., BSP/1/8,
    p. 49.
100 ibid., p. 66.
101 Minutes of municipal council, 18
    March 1865–5 March 1866,
    D.C.A., C2/A1/26, p. 238.
102 Pim to Butt, 27 June, 1873, N.L.I.,
    Butt papers, MS. 10415 (4).
103 *Bill to amend law relating to superan-
    nuation of prison officers in Ireland*,
    H.C., 1873 (142) iv. 225.
104 See note 110 below.
105 Mostyn to inspectors-general, 21
    Jan. 1868, N.A., C.C.S. 1868,
    no.321.
106 Gregg to Mosyn, 21 Jan 1868,
    N.A., C.C.S. 1868, no.321.
107 *F. J.*, 9 Feb 1869.
108 Leon O Broin, *Fenian fever, an
    Anglo-Irish dilemma*, (London,
    1971), pp 26–9.
109 *F. J.*, 9 Feb 1869.
110 J. Lawless (?) to Synnott, 1 Nov.
    1876, N.L., Butt papers, MS. 8706.
111 Probate of 'the last will and testa-
    ment and codicil of Mrs. Marian
    Synnott', 1870, N.A., T. 9175. See
    also *Wills and administrations*, N.A.,
    1870, p. 542.
112 Registry of deaths, Dublin, 17
    Dec. 1897, Registry of births,
    deaths and marriages, Vol. 2, p. 432.
113 MS. in possession of Brian
    Siggons, Sandymount, Dublin.

CONCLUSION

1 *Dublin prisons board report*, (Dublin,
    1869), pp 60–1.
2 *Forty-second report on general state of
    prisons of Ireland*, H.C., 1864
    [3377], xxvii, pp 402–3.